6-2-64

ID0983847

CHRISTIAN
ETHICS
AND
THE SIT-IN

BOOKS BY PAUL RAMSEY

Basic Christian Ethics

Faith and Ethics:
  The Theology of H. Richard Niebuhr *(Editor)*

Freedom of the Will, by Jonathan Edwards *(Editor)*

War and the Christian Conscience

CHRISTIAN ETHICS AND THE SIT=IN

by

PAUL RAMSEY

ASSOCIATION PRESS · **NEW YORK**

CHRISTIAN ETHICS AND THE SIT-IN

———

DEDICATED TO MY DAUGHTER

MARCIA NEAL RAMSEY

WHO FIRST ARRIVED AT THE AGE OF

DISCRETION IN THESE MATTERS, AND

THEN WENT OFF TO COLLEGE

Contents

Introduction

There is a stirring in this land. The dedicated young men and young women who are participating in the sit-ins at lunch counters have placed their fellow citizens and fellow Christians on notice that we have not achieved the future rapidly enough. We have not attained that greater justice in the common life of this nation and general recognition of the human dignity of non-white people that is theirs by right and that is bound to come in fact. During the Roosevelt era, Negroes advanced primarily in economic status. During the Truman and the Eisenhower periods their gains have been more in sharing in our political life and in civil rights. Perhaps the crest of this development, and certainly the most dramatic symbol of it, was the 1954 Supreme Court decision declaring unconstitutional any enforced segregation of pupils according to race in the public schools, and the subsequent implementation of this decision in many school districts.

The adjustment of our practices in education to this decision has been an ordeal that is still going on in many quarters, while in others, albeit under legal pressure, wisdom and moderation have been forthcoming on the part of community leaders and white and Negro people alike. Still, in any over-all view of the matter, there has been more deliberateness than speed even in attaining the justice that now is guaranteed by law. Perhaps this was necessary when one considers the magnitude of the change this called for in people's attitudes and practices which had the force of long-standing social habit. Yet, both in right and law such gradualism as we have seen should not have been necessary. Too much desegregation has been token only, and in some states the deliberate steps speedily taken have been to the end of frustrating rather than implementing the Court's decision.

In this context we have to understand the recent sit-ins and other forms of direct, non-violent action, such as boycotts of segregating public transportation systems. This shows quite understandable and justifiable impatience on the part of young Negroes—the so-called "new" Negroes—who have finally disproved the white man's contention that the Negro is happiest with inequality or under enforced separation. Even the step by step, legal precedent by precedent, procedures of the National Association for the Advancement of Colored People no longer seem the only way to full citizenship. Therefore young Negro college students on their own, at first spontaneously and then as an organized movement, challenged by direct action the conscience of the white man to respect and act in accord with the rights that properly belong to them as men. Several generations have been long enough to wait for justice; and five years since the highest court ruled on desegregation of the schools now seems too long to wait for what is legally their due.

Negro students have been joined in some instances

by whites. They go to segregated lunch counters and there with quiet courage wait to be served. They have endured public insult yet steadfastly refused to leave. While not exactly turning the other cheek, some of these young people have had lighted cigarettes pressed upon their flesh and they have refrained from striking back in retaliation. Arrested they refuse bail. In some southern cities the leaders of the community have led the way in opening lunch counters to everyone without regard to race. In others, legal cases have started through the courts after the Negroes were arrested and their defense taken up by the NAACP or the American Civil Liberties Union. In still other localities and states, new legislation has been enacted to make it clearly illegal to remain on business property when requested to leave. It is to be expected that these ambiguous consequences will continue. In some places customs of segregation will fall like a house of cards when pushed hard enough. In others the lines of separation will be hardened and the legal definition of the rights of the owners of private property will be fixed more securely for a time. It is therefore to be expected that sit-ins will continue, and that this mode of public protest and direct action to change social practices will be used in more localities and against additional forms of racial discrimination where reform is urgently needed.

These young people sitting there without a mumbling word nevertheless speak. They speak for man. They speak for man to men. They speak to men about what all men owe one another. They also speak as Christians. They speak concerning what Christians owe to all men and to one another. The sit-in is therefore not only a stirring in this land. It is also a stirring in the Christian church—a challenge to man, a challenge also to the church. The challenge of their presence and determination plainly springs from deep Christian as well as human impulses. The leaders of the Southern Christian Leadership Conference and many of the leaders of the Committee on Racial Equality (CORE) understand the sit-in movement as a form of Christian action. Theirs is not simply a program or goal. Theirs also is a spirit and a mode of conduct that aims to include respect for the persons whose practice they oppose. No one can read Martin Luther King's *Stride toward Freedom* or James M. Lawson, Jr.'s forthcoming book on non-violence without acknowledging the Christian intent as well as the social protest at work here. The same must indubitably be said when one hears of the planning and training sessions often held in churches, in which sit-ins are simulated and the opposition dramatized, in order that the participants can learn how to respond under extreme provocation, and how when reviled not to revile again. May it not be that these young people are guilty only of performing an effective Christian deed? That they have merely begun to transform the social order more rapidly than this can be done by law alone?

Nevertheless, there is a place for reflective examination of any social movement and for self-examination even in the best of causes. This is true whether the sit-in movement is regarded as a form of political action or a form of Christian action. In both cases, criticism and discussion are always prerequisite to a wise pursuit of the common good or of a good in common. Democracy rests upon the conviction that the truth men need to know and apply precisely in this hour they can progressively discover through unrestricted discussion. Government by the consent of the governed really means by the consent of an informed people; and this in turn means by the consent of a people who inform and listen to one another. This book is a small contribution to the discussion that can and may and must go on among people of many and all different points of view if the decisions made and actions taken in our society are to be sound ones.

It is also a small contribution to the discussion that can and may and must go on in the church among Christians about this particular movement called the sit-ins as a form of Christian action in race relations. Here again there is a place for criticism and reflective examination and interchanged views. The people of God are no less than a congregation of people who individually and corporately discipline themselves under the guidance of the Holy Spirit, who will lead us into all truth. Here, too, every man must say what it is given him to see and to think, lest others lose by his silence. Striving to speak the truth in love, Christians have witness to bear to one another concerning the meaning of Jesus Christ precisely in this hour and for the actualities comprising the full range of human affairs today. This is one meaning of the priesthood of all believers *to each other*. This means that not even for the sake of united action can there be any arbitrary limit placed on reflective examination of the issues, or upon self-examination. If the attitudes expressed and the decisions taken from within the Christian church are to be sound ones, everyone should be willing to be an examiner and to instruct others as well as examine his own point of view constantly in the light of the reports of other witnesses. Therefore, this volume is intended to be a small item in the discussion of the vital issues of race relations which should be going on in our society wherever citizens, and in the churches wherever disciples of Christ, are urgently seeking to find the truth to be done.

For it cannot be denied that concerning the sit-ins and race relations and almost every other subject under the sun, too much is said by too many too lightly. The same is true of what is said about the rights of property owners. Direct action in the sit-ins has been both condemned and praised without prior analysis of some of the deeper issues involved. Suddenly confronted by a resolute sit-in group capable of preventing normal service at lunch counters unless and until food is served without discrimination as to race, many people see in this only a "lawless" action and the threat of anarchy if established institutions and customs are breached. Until forced to do so, they do not inquire into the fundamental meaning of justice which, in the nature of the case, is invoked by this action.

On the other hand, the sit-ins are widely approved—by politicians with their eyes on blocks of votes and by Christians and others with an eye only for simple justice. College and seminary teachers of the older generation, who were brought up on causes and whose fondest memories are of times they went out on picket lines, may be overheard to say that in this age of conformity they are glad to see their students excited about *something.* Just as those who too quickly condemn the sit-ins need to think more deeply about the meaning of justice, so those who are too facile in approval of them may need to think more deeply about the problems of law and public order.

Such issues as these are dealt with in this book. In the first chapter, on the created destination of property right, we shall attempt to uncover the meaning of that natural justice which *should* be exhibited in our laws. In the second, the moral issues involved in law observance and civil disobedience are taken up. These two chapters together expound a philosophy of law resting both on natural justice and, secondarily, on the need for order. The final chapter deals with morality and the broader use of economic pressures, boycotts, etc. as a means of transforming race relations.

These subjects are approached from the point of view of Christian social ethics. This requires that property rights, the sit-ins, and indeed problems in race relations generally, have to be apprehended in terms of the basic concepts of Christian theological ethics. For example, God's creation of human beings for covenant, and human nature as "fellow humanity," are fundamental to any proper understanding of that natural justice on which rest our laws. The distance and yet the relation between man and man which fellow humanity requires may afford a criterion for an assessment of our laws of property.

At the same time, the Christian understanding of the fallen creation and its *always already* broken covenants gives the justification for a regard for order as well as for justice on which any good society must be founded. Throughout, the illumination and transformation of justice by love, and the consequent interlacing of the order of justice and the order of charity, in both of which the Christian lives, are sought to be made clear. Along the way, objection is raised against the identification of Christian action *as such* with non-violent resistance. Although this seems to be the opinion of many leaders of the sit-ins, and in spite of the fact that it underlies very much that is most admirable in the spirit of the participants, this identification is still a mistaken account of Christian ethics in practice. Concerning non-violent resistance, like any other act of resistance, the Christian must ask whether any such thing is permitted and required by Christian love. And as with any other tactical action appearing in the public sphere, its justice and its lawfulness must be subjected to inquiry by the Christian and the responsible citizen.

In the final analysis, therefore, the theme of this volume is as much the nature and meaning of Christian ethics as the nature and meaning of the sit-ins or justice in race relations. At least, he should read no further who expects a sociological treatment or a political tract. But there is nothing wrong with a study of the sit-ins which proposes at the same time to be a study of Christian ethics, or vice versa. No moral outlook is more oriented toward practice, no ethics more bound to fulfill itself in action. On the other hand, no deed and no concrete social movement can be said to fall outside of God's world, or outside of the world the reality of which is most fully grasped and penetrated by means of the principles of Christian theological ethics.

Therefore, Christian ethics as a *theory* is always an interruption of Christian action—not, like philosophical ethics today, an interruption of *talk,* talking merely about talk about ethical conduct. This book proposes to interrupt or intervene in the action of the sit-ins for the purpose of reflecting ethically and Christianly about them, and about race relations. It is not surprising that in this moment of reflection upon a specific moral or political action, the whole cosmos of Christian ethics should become pertinent to the discussion. This needs to be brought to bear not only upon the action of the sit-in participants, but also upon the more constant procedures of white property owners, legislators, and the political leaders of the white community, and upon all our laws and customs. For this reason, the chapter on the created destination of property right is placed *first* in this book, with its proposed intervention in conceptions of the absolute rights of the individual. Such notions need fundamental review and reconstruction.

If this seems to rank reflection and discussion or criticism too highly, let me say that I am sure that all this is at most only the little finger on the body of Christ. I am confident that God can make the un-self-critical deeds of noble and courageous men to praise him, and even unexamined lives worth living. In particular, I hope that no reader of this book supposes I only want to freeze history or temper action in order to make sure it is ethical enough. Rather is it the case that in obedience to Jesus Christ and in covenant with him with all men, the agent and the thinker are one.

Every Christian is to some degree a Christian ethicist. This means that the Christian who is most engaged in social action must sometimes interrupt himself in order the better to understand what he is doing and to know the obedience he is called to perform. He intervenes in his own course of action and makes judgments upon it. This book simply sets forth what such a Christian man may and should say in a moment of reflection upon the totality of his action in the cause of justice and human rights.

My colleague, Professor Malcolm Diamond, in the Department of Religion at Princeton University, Professor J. Robert Nelson, formerly Dean of the School of Religion at Vanderbilt University and Visiting Professor at Princeton Theological Seminary during 1961-62, and the Reverend Thomas Bennett, YMCA Secretary for Public Affairs, Christian Emphasis, and Church Co-operation, read the manuscript of this book, and gave me the benefits of their criticisms and suggestions. I am also grateful to the Reverend Cameron P. Hall, Executive Director of the Department of the Church and Economic Life of the National Council of the Churches of Christ in the U.S.A., for initially stimulating me in this study; and to the members of the General Commission on the Church and Economic Life, on which I serve, who heard a brief report of it and many of whom did not agree.

PAUL RAMSEY
Department of Religion
Princeton University

1

The Created Destination of Property Right

The sit-ins have raised basic questions concerning law and concerning civil rights. In common justice, the right of property in our law either is or should be the "inn keeper's law" in the tradition of the Anglo-Saxon common law. Whether this *is* our law of quasi-public property is, as we shall see, a question secondary in importance only to the question what the law *should* be if it is just. But first, why should the law governing property rights express the "inn keeper's law?"

This rule stated that whoever opened an inn or tavern serving travelers with bed and food should not then discriminate among those who apply for these services he is in business to sell, and that in the possession and use of such private property he should not turn anyone away for whom he had room. That was property right as a form of fellow humanity. It meant that certain forms of property were to be destined by their owners to the common good in the service of the concrete needs of men without arbitrary distinctions. The rule was soundly based on the abstract equality of man *with* fellow man; and since this also entailed no small measure of distributive justice that took into account the concrete nature of one's fellow man, it was therefore also based squarely upon the owner's nature as a man *for* other men, and upon property right as an expression of fellow humanity.

Here was none of that erroneous notion that a man without his fellow man, and with no duties toward him, can be the bearer of absolute rights and use property in any way he pleases. The "inn keeper's law" said in effect that all must be served by any man who sets up an inn at the crossroads that weary travellers reach by nightfall, since, having established himself there as owner, he now occupies the space that otherwise might be held by an owner whose practice would be more in accord with natural justice or with the requirements of man's life with man. Man's destiny as a creature made in the image of God—in the image of God's fellow humanity—affects any of those inalienable rights he may be said to possess. Property right, and the uses of space and position on the earth in which man is given to dwell but over which no man gains *dominion*—these are in order to man in the time of his covenant with fellow man. Whether the owner knows this or not, and even if he may never say *Thou* to all or to any of his paying guests, his own humanity in its creation, and therefore the fashion of any rights he inalienably possesses, have imprinted on them the destiny toward which he was made. The "inn keeper's law" manifests the fact that the political order with its justice and its law and a man's proper relation to the things he owns are the external basis, the promise, the possibility and capability for covenant-community.

This probes the situation more deeply than did Governor LeRoy Collins in his commendable statement that while Negroes may not have a "legal" right in some states to be served at segregated lunch-counters, they have a "moral" right to be served in any part of an establishment whose proprietor invites them to buy goods from him in another part. Property right as a form of fellow humanity expresses more clearly why this is true, and *that* it is unquestionably true, if our rules of law succeed in instituting that justice which is natural to man. This applies also to the ownership rights of a restaurant proprietor or hotel manager who may have no other business on the premises into which he ever invites a certain class or kind of people. Collins' statement says nothing wrong, but it says not enough. So also Martin Luther King's assertion (after affirming his belief in "basic rights that should be protected concerning private property") that "we are not dealing with property that is exclusively private. We are dealing with property that is privately owned but supported by, sustained by the public and which depends on the public for its very existence...."[1] If it is only hospitality that is violated when an owner trades with some people he declines to serve at a lunch counter as long as they are willing to trade on this basis, and if only the public's support of his business warrants the owner's returning their favor, then presumably he might be justified in selecting a part of the public he is in business to serve, or to serve in some part but not in all parts of his establishment. Justice in practice rests not simply on elementary fairness, but on the created desti-

----

[1] "Are Sit-In Strikes Justifiable," *The Nation's Future*, NBC-TV, November 2, 1960. King's statement that "individuals who are in the common market with their stores should not deny individuals access to the common market" comes closest to the point. Nor should the law allow this.

nation of property as a whole to the good of fellow humanity. Even in our more populous and complex society, it may be said that, if a person who bears the human countenance arrives weary from shopping for her family and beset by two tired and thirsty children at a place on the earth where drink and food are offered for purchase, the owner of this place cannot turn her away without doing violence to the just cause among men. It is due to all who come now to this place to know that they have not gone out of the world in which God and man have time for them. Having established himself there as owner he now occupies the space that otherwise might be held by an owner whose practice would, at the very *time* it is needed *there*, be more in accord with man's life with man. This still holds in principle, to define the right of property in union with its destination, even if there are no other persons in the vicinity as potential proprietors of whom our courts can take judicial notice who would in fact come into the possession of this property and, so far, of their own humanity in the form of fellow humanity.

Natural Justice and Charity

We can also see in this why the same may not apply to all the property to which men have title. It is certainly the case that I may invite some people into some parts of my home while not opening other parts or the whole of it to them; and, so far as the law and justice alone are concerned, in doing this I may discriminate among kinds or races of people. My momentary obligation clearly does not allow this when Christ appears at my door disguised as the hungry, the thirsty, the homeless, or the naked. That, however, is a matter of charity, and of love-transformed-justice pressing home the full meaning of man's life for man as Christ was for us. Yet even if I see my neighbors as Christs to me, still I do not generalize this to mean every man's natural right at any time to be provisioned with whatever my home supplies to any, as should be the rule in regard to the use of things and places on the earth for many business, if these are public, purposes. In the one case the distance between I and Thou is given external support; in the other, a relation is externally guaranteed to me and in me to every Thou. In the one case a measure of privacy that enables one to do what he will with his own has meaning and gives important support to a man's being a fellow man at all; in the case of the "inn keeper's law" there is externally grounded the necessity that he shall be this at least in some minimal fashion, and the fact is expressed that in common justice a man has no natural right to attempt to be a man wholly in isolation from his fellow man in the use of the things he owns. Both uses of property, or both definitions of the rights of property, are necessary to fellow humanity in that both sustain externally the capacity for covenant and give real promise of this. In the one, the stress is upon the fact that I need not be absorbed into my relationships; in the other, the stress is upon the fact that I am not myself, i.e., not an I, unless, if only in some minimal way, I say Thou, and own things in order to be with and for fellow man.

As we seek to promote justice among men, Christian thought and practice should be deeply concerned over what may happen to the Thou who is every man if this is understood in terms of absolute rights of property and laws of property whose justice presupposes a man may be without fellow man. We should also be equally concerned over what may happen to the I who is every man if this comes under an only abstract justice or equality and ways of forcing men by law to be with and for others. This latter point calls for treatment later on. But first the basis in creation (or in natural justice) for the destination of property in unbreakable covenant with fellow man should be fully explored.

Karl Barth has written that, in the Christian view, creation is the external basis of covenant, creation is the promise and makes possible the history of God's covenant dealings with mankind; while His covenant is the internal basis, the meaning or purpose of creation.[2] An illustration of this can immediately be given: human sexuality, in its created nature, is to be understood properly as no individual matter, and certainly not as a mere biological fact, but as the external basis, the promise and possibility of the marriage covenant and the capability of nature for fellow humanity between man and woman, and as such this is an effective token and *image,* in fact *the* image, of God's covenant and fellow humanity with man; viewed in the other direction, the ordinance, law, or covenant of marriage is the internal basis and meaning or purpose of created human sexuality.[3]

---

[2] *Church Dogmatics* (Edinburgh: T. & T. Clark, 1958), III, 1, Sec. 41, 2, 3.

[3] Cf. *Ibid.,* III, 1, Sec. 41, 2 (pp. 288-329), and III, 2, Sec. 45, 3 (pp. 285-324). In the language and in the substance of what follows in

It is worth noting, parenthetically, that sexual differentiation or the duality of man and woman is the primary form of fellow humanity and the only indestructible image of covenant in which man was created. By contrast,

> the so-called races of mankind are only variations of one and the same structure, allowing at any time the practical intermingling of the one with the other and consisting only in fleeting transitions from the one to the other. . . . In the distinction of man and woman, however, we have a structural differentiation of human existence. . . . His creatureliness is to be male or female, male and female, and human in this distinction and connection. He certainly exists in other essential and non-essential differentiations. He is necessarily a child, and this individual as opposed to others. But these distinctions as such are not structural in character. . . . He does not need to be father or mother, brother or sister, young or old, gifted or not gifted, endowed in this way or that, a man of this or that particular time or sphere or race. . . . In and with his existence as a man, and as this particular man, he is male or female, male and female. And in and with all the other essen-

---

this section I am, of course, greatly indebted to Karl Barth. His theological reflection goes before and after mine, as mine goes before (since I, too, have the Bible) and gratefully after his.

The development of a philosophy of law and an analysis of "natural" justice on the basis of covenant-creation is imperative even for a Barthian theological ethics. It is not enough simply to speak of "church law," or the human law developed within the community of believers, as "exemplary law" that may provide indirect guidance for the political order where "some form of law is sought and found, in an attempted movement from the worse to better" (*C-D*, IV, 2, Sec. 67, 4, p. 722). Before and while this may be true, creation-covenant may provide criteria for this movement of secular law from worse to better. To show how this is so is a task for theological ethics—if, as Barth everywhere insists, Christology is not creation or anthropology, and anthropology or the doctrine of creation are not Christology.

tial and non-essential distinctions and connections, this is decisive and in a sense exemplary because this alone is structural and runs through all the others, maintaining, expressing and revealing itself in them. In all the common and opposing features of human existence, there is no man in isolation, but only man or woman, man and woman. In the whole reach of human life there is no abstractly human but only concretely masculine or feminine being, feeling, willing, thinking, speaking, conduct and action, and only concretely masculine and feminine co-existence and co-operation in all these things.[4]

From the primacy of the man-woman form of fellow humanity, or of the marks in sexuality of our creation for covenant, two conclusions may be drawn relevant to race relations:

1. No human law should attempt to put asunder what God has joined together, as is sought to be done by the antimiscegenation laws of many states prohibiting interracial marriages. As the Supreme Court of California said in declaring that state's antimiscegenation law unconstitutional, while a state has the power and the duty to regulate marriage, if its marriage law is "discriminatory and irrational, it unconstitutionally restricts not only religious liberty but the liberty to marry as well."[5] This 1948 decision involved petitioners of different races who were also Roman Catholics and who contended that the laws in question were unconstitutional, on the grounds, among others, that they prohibited the free exercise of their religion and

---

[4] *Ibid.*, III, 2, Sec. 45, p. 286.
[5] *Perez v. Sharp*, 32 Cal. 2d 711, 198 P. 2d 17.

denied to them the right to participate fully in the sacraments of that religion.

2. On the other hand, we are not bidden by our Creator to ignore the greater ultimacy of the creation of male and female in attempting to refashion race relations to accord more with fellow humanity. To point to the fact that the danger of intermarriage has been used by misguided white people as only a subterfuge for denying elementary justice in race relations, to recall the exploitive sexual coercion of Negro women in the past by white men, and to demonstrate, quite correctly, that social intimacy and the freedom of marriage are not what is mainly wanting or at all wanted in greater justice in the relations between the races, will not be sufficient to create an abstract manhood in place of the man-womanhood God has made. Sexuality is in us His summons to fellow humanity, and where two or three are gathered together with equality and justice in other respects this summons may be expected to be heard. On all sides, this has to be acknowledged and taken realistically into account, lest, because of the sins of their fathers, our children's covenants be set on edge in the years to come.

In the very nature of human sexuality, then, are marks of the indestructible force of our creation in and for fellow humanity, and of the destination of sex to our existence in covenant. This can also be expressed at once in broader social ethical terms. The state and its law as an ordinance of creation, natural justice, human and legal rights, and social institutions generally, so far as these have a positive purpose under the creative, governing, and preserving purposes of God—

all are the external basis making possible the actualization of the promise of covenant; while covenant or fellow humanity is the internal basis and meaning of every right, true justice, or law. This enables us to see why the requirements of charity, or of steadfast covenant-love, and the requirements of justice, or of natural right, are ultimately inseverable. Each conditions the other, and we are told that what is required of us is only to do justice [the justice that provides an in-principled expression of divine charity or gives external basis for or promise of, or prepares in the desert a highway for God's mercy] and to love mercy [the mercy that determinately fashions our human justice] and to walk humbly in covenant with our God (Mic. 6:8).

This can be understood even more closely in the following way. In the order of charity the Christian is able and free to be, and therefore he should be, *for* other men, as Jesus Christ was *the* man *for* his fellow man and, as such, "the image of the invisible God" (*Col.* 1:15) or the image of that fellow humanity in which God elected Himself from the foundations of the world to be for man and resolved not without man to be God. In *this* God's very image Adam and in him all men were originally made in and for their own fellow humanity. Natural justice however, is far less than this. Justice bears only the external marks of man's destiny for steadfast covenant-love. It provides only the external possibility of covenant, or a minimum sign and promise of this. Perhaps, therefore, the fellow humanity of man that shows forth in the order of justice can best be described as the life of man *with* fellow man (not *for* him). Yet, to be *for* fellow man (charity) and to be *with* fellow man (justice) indicates the permeability of justice to charity. Charity (*for* fellow man) is the internal basis and meaning of natural justice (*with* fellow man), as justice in turn is the promise and possibility of closer meeting and steadfast covenant. This has to be said of every human right, e.g., property, of which we speak in Christian social ethics. Human rights all bear the marks of the primal justice of man's creation for fellow humanity; and property should manifest the fact that a man alone is not God's creature. Rights such as those of ownership should reflect the just cause among men (man *with* man), and man's destination for fellow humanity.

Man *with* man entails, at the minimum, a rather external system of relationships according to which each is given his exact due and regarded as abstractly equal to any other man before the law. The life of man *with* man requires at least that Aristotle's corrective or arithmetical justice be socially enforced. This we usually call "equality before the law." So "it makes no difference whether a robbery, for instance, is committed by a good man on a bad or by a bad man on a good," or by a rich man on a poor man or a Negro on a white man, or vice versa:

> the law looks only to the difference created by the injury and treats the men as previously equal, where the one does and the other suffers injury, or the one has done and the other suffered harm. . . . So it is the office of a judge to make things equal, and the line, as it were, having been unequally divided, he takes from the greater part that by which it exceeds the half, and adds this on to the less. And when the whole is divided

into two exactly equal portions then men say they have their own. . . .[6]

Yet natural justice can be stretched, converted, or elevated when it is permeated by the spirit of charity. Natural justice itself shows evidence of this. For man *with* man entails also a closer and more perceptive relation with him that takes account of inequalities and the concrete details of his actual being and situation. This is man *with* man in the form of Aristotle's proportionate or distributive justice, and finally as equity. In concrete human relationships abstract equality is not enough. Justice requires also that individual differences be taken into account. The bonds of social union and reciprocation must be "according to proportion and not exact equality" alone.[7] For Aristotle this meant that "if the persons are not equal they must not have equal shares,"[8] and that in any "division made out of common property, the shares will bear the same proportion to one another as the original contributions did."[9] Because such justice faces the concrete persons and acknowledges their differences, it is susceptible of infusion by charity, by which the life of man *with* fellow man begins to assume more of a Christian form in proportioning justice for men by distributing to them in accordance with their need for help and rescue. This is a love-transformed-justice, which decides the crucial issue remaining for natural justice, i.e., whether the just community among men shall be con-

---

[6] Aristotle, *Ethics*, 1132a.
[7] *Ibid.*, 1132b.
[8] *Ibid.*, 1131a.
[9] *Ibid.*, 1131b.

strued largely as honoring the greatest contributors to the common weal in their inequality with others, or more largely as bending the system of relations of man *with* and (so far as may be) his life *for* fellow man in the direction of succor for the lowliest in their inequality with others.

It is in the administration of *equity* that charity can clearly make itself felt in the order of justice. For Aristotel defines the equitable as "a correction of the law, where the law is defective by reason of its universality."[10] It is not only just to be equitable in correcting the law by sometimes making an exception in applying it to concrete cases. Considerations of equity can also provide a growing edge in the law itself, correcting, improving and humanizing it by first transforming the universalities of man's understanding of justice. So equity can correct justice, provided there is guidance for equity to be found in charity and if equity is not confined to making justice only more just in practice. Yet even Aristotle knew that justice had finally to be co-extensive with perfect virtue. Justice, fully developed and applied, and perfect virtue are "the same really, but the point of view is not the same: in so far as it has respect to one's neighbor it is justice; in so far as it is such and such a moral state it is simply virtue."[11] In order for this to be entirely acceptable to the Christian, he has simply to say that in so far as charity has respect to his neighbor it is justice brought to final completion, or the life of man *with* man transformed, through the illumination of equity, into the

---

10 *Ibid.*, 1137b.
11 *Ibid.*, 1130a.

covenant life of man *for* man. Thus from the beginning, to be *with* fellow man within the structures of law and institutions provides the external basis, the promise and pledge or the possibility of covenant-love *for* him; in being *for* fellow man is revealed the internal basis of any sort of justice, or the meaning and intentionality there were present all along in that life of man *with* man which God directs in creating, preserving, and governing the world by means of the social order. His rights are a man's capability to covenant. Man was made, with all his rights, to be claimed for covenant, and to have and exercise his rights with and for fellow humanity. In covenant was every man made from his birth, and without fellow humanity was not anything made that was made—no man, no rights of his, no justice, no proper law.

Property and Creation-Covenant

Let the reader be encouraged if the foregoing seems obscure enough to be theologically profound. For it is now time to take up again the question of property and so-called ownership rights as such. From the point of view of the Christian understanding of creation-covenant, man's propensity to sin is exhibited not only in the isolation of his often wanting to be without fellow man or in imperialism against his fellow man and wanting him to be for self. It is exhibited also in the way we put ourselves forward to be with him, and in our claims for justice or rights in relation to him and his. Christians acknowledge how flimsy is the right and how questionable the justice we claim to be the bearers of apart from or only halfheartedly in covenant relation. Yet sinful man affirms that, as an individual item, he has his humanity, his natural and human rights and justice due him, radically without his fellow man, half without him, and on some other basis than a man's own true manhood *with* other men. He claims to possess absolute rights, say, to life, or happiness, or property—adding perhaps that he will doubtless share some corner of these just possessions of his with, and in some degree make sovereign use of them for, his fellow man. Thus, a man in isolation with his rights and his just dues comes *first;* and on the basis of this, it is hoped, a surrogate for covenant may be established as a sort of bargain or contract by which an individual by his own will agrees to put himself into some measure of responsible relation with and for his fellow man, arbitrarily or according as it is in his own best interest to do so.

This is a basically mistaken view of justice and of human rights, because it is a mistaken view of God's creation in man. A man is never without his fellow man in any such fashion, nor does he reach his neighbor only by choice or contract from which he can as easily withdraw. Instead, because his creatureliness is from the beginning in the form of fellow humanity and because the creation in him is in order to covenant, and because this means he has real being only by being *with* and *for* fellow man, we have to reckon with this in everything that is said about justice and about the rights of man. His rights have their being in, with, and for covenant. The rights of man are the rights of the fellow humanity of those who bear them. If, for example, ownership and use of property is a right it is a human right (and not therefore to be sharply contrasted with "human rights"), and property as a human and not an impersonal thing means from the beginning, or, as it were, from the bottom up, that it is a right inhering in human nature because this has the form of fellow humanity. Property, like other rights, is the promise and the possibility; it is a man's capability for life *for* and *with* his fellow man, that is, it is the external basis of covenant, if we are to say in Christian social theory that it is a "natural" right based on the structure of God's creation.

This is the reason for, and a far more adequate account of, the so-called "social reservation" it has been necessary to introduce into more individualistic theories of the rights of man in order to give rise or effect at all to the duties of man. Thus, a man and his father before him, in the comparatively small kingdom of Denmark, may have "owned" a tree for many, many years. Yet it never becomes theirs to use as they please, an absolute property right. They may not cut it down without showing that they have specifically remembered and cared that they are men with other men now living, and with their children's children for generations yet to come who need and will continue to have need for trees to be in Denmark, no matter who says he owns them. The public authority, in this instance, stands ready to direct any exercise of individual right of ownership to, with, and for the owner's fellow man. This is a better way to express the "social reservation" and the duties of men in the midst of the rights they possess, than to say (with traditional Aristotelian-Thomistic social philosophy) that, while at its heart the *ownership* of property is a private right, it *use* must be directed (either by the owner's action or, absent that, by the state) to the common good. That is a patchwork, which says that man is man first primarily apart from fellow man in one aspect of property (ownership, or *dominion*), yet at the same time and also primarily a man with his fellow man in another aspect of it (use).

Ours is a better formulation because it is based on a unifying biblical understanding of creation-covenant, and accordingly on a man and his rights always and from the beginning having the form of fellow humanity. The right of property means the stewardship of property (of which man never has *dominion,* private or otherwise); and stewardship means that a thing may be ours in that we are persons in covenant, and that property should be held and used in fealty toward God and in recognition of His sovereign right and sole dominion and, indivisible from this, it should be held and used in fealty of life with our fellow men.

Men need property *not* because the status of their private personalities, as individual embodied persons, is precarious in them unless they have a special space or room in which to exercise the private dominion and management of their reasons over physical things. They need property and things because the status of *fellow humanity* is precarious in them. Men have a right to private property not because they mixed their reasons and wills with nature or, by individual labor, carved their own out of the state of nature where all things were once common. Nor certainly do they have a right to private property only as a grant from the state.[12] They have a right to private property and the direction of things because this is a necessary and desirable part of their created life in fellow humanity with and for fellow man. By contrast, the angels need no property—not because they are unembodied spirits needing no physical place in which to live nor because the status, development, and exercise of their spiritual natures are not made precarious by or suffer threat from dependence on physical things. They need no property because God created each angel a separate complete species with no fellows, entirely complete in himself, a specific individual unlike any others and a

---

[12] An interpretation of property right based on creation-covenant escapes the extremes of individualism or collectivism, or the extremes of the absolute right of private ownership or the absolute right of society to direct these owners. On the one hand, John Locke's individualistic justification of property as a natural right "without any express compact of all the commoners" has to be rejected, along with his account of the origin of private property: "Whatsoever, then, he removes out of the state that nature hath provided and left it in, *he hath mixed his labor with,* and joined to it something that is his own, and thereby makes it his property. It being by him removed from the common state nature placed it in, it hath by this labor something annexed to it *that excludes the common right of other men.* For this labor being the unquestionable property of the laborer, no man but he can have a right to what that is once joined to"—to which some provision for the common good can only be externally appended, as when Locke continues: "at least where there is enough, and as good left in common for others" to appropriate by their own isolated labors *(Second Treatise on Civil Government,* Ch. V, pars. 25, 27, italics added). On the other hand, J. J. Rousseau's exclusively social derivation of property right has equally to be rejected. "The first man," Rousseau wrote ironically, "who, having enclosed a piece of ground, bethought himself of saying *This is mine,* and found people simple enough to believe him, was the real founder of civil society. . . . It was in vain to repeat, 'I built this well; I gained this spot by my industry.' Who gave you your standing, it might be answered, and what right have you to demand payment of us for doing what we never asked you to do?" *(A Discourse on the Origin of Inequality,* Pt. II, Everyman ed., pp. 207, 220). Thus, an understanding of human nature as nature created in and for covenant is the foundation of any sound political or social theory, and of the natural rights of men indivisible from the duties of fellow humanity.

being of which there are no other instances, whose thought goes swiftly to the point without need for circuitous reasoning or for any community of searching discourse with other angels, and who live always directly in the praise of God. (The angels only sing, as it happens together, but each in his own kind. Their harmony is predetermined, like the music of the spheres they were formerly supposed to inhabit, and their praise is not a matter of covenant-response. They do not sing *with* fellow angels, or have any other life with them. They are not creatures of the Covenant.[13]) Man, however, has been placed a little higher than the angels[14] in that God created him over against himself as His own special covenant partner and created him in the very image of this same covenant partnership (of God with and for man) by giving him a humanity whose nature consists of partnership with fellow man. Everything that is said about rights, e.g., property, and about law and justice must take this fundamentally into account.

Man has rights because fellow humanity is precarious in him. How shall this be understood? The covenant is not a relationship with disappearing terms. It is not a pure internal relation with no irreducibly different beings to be related to each other. There is distance in the relation, and relatedness in the dis-

---

[13] The writer agrees with the statement that whoever has not meditated much on God, the angels, and the *summum bonum* may possibly make a thriving earthworm, but not very much of a man.

[14] The familiar verse in Ps. 8:5 in praise of the gifts with which God has shown he is mindful of man, "Thou hast made him a little lower than the angels," reads instead in the Hebrew, "Thou hast made him a little lower than God [or, to lack something from God, or the gods], and crowned him with glory and honor."

tance. Thus, the idea of *covenant*-bond stands between or beyond the idea of *contract* (in which only the surfaces of selves are engaged in action with one another), on one hand, and, on the other, the idea of *union* or merger of beings. This is clear enough in the case of God and man. God does not unite or blend his nature with man's; He covenants with him, holding him in a life-in-community in which God remains irreducibly other than man and man a creature not himself in any sense divine. I can say Thou to God only if I am maintained in difference from him as an independent creature; yet I could never say Thou to God unless this expressed the fact that in my being, however independent, I am always with and for Him, based on no will or deed of my own but on the fact that He is *my* God, i.e., because, as Christians affirm, from all eternity He is Christ for us and has bound himself not ever to be God without us.

But this is not nearly so clear in regard to man's fellow humanity *with man*. How can I avoid the defect of meeting him only in incidental, contractual ways, with only a part of my being engaged in this, without falling into either the submissive excess of identifying myself with him or the imperialistic excess of identifying him with me? How can I have the strength to be irreducibly other than he is, and to allow him to be other than I am, and yet live with and for him from my heart? How can I be I who am I only in saying Thou to him? How can he be himself a self who has his very being only in fellow humanity with me? How can there be distance maintained without rupturing our fellow humanity? How can there

be real relations between us without loss of the dis-
tinctiveness of each? In Tillich's terms, how can I have
the courage to accomplish the movement in my existence of being apart, and simultaneously have the
courage to accomplish the movement of being a part?[15]

We speak not of the courage and the faith to do
this, but of the importance and the function of human
rights in the social order based on creation and legally
defined as the promise and the substantial possibility
of our doing this, or as the external basis for covenant.
If human rights are the rights of fellow humanity, "inalienably" connected with this human nature in us
and with our life with fellow man and with our duties
to other men, then rights must be whatever it is necessary for me to have in order to be with and for fellow
man. If I have an inalienable, natural right to life
simply by my being a man, this is because life is the
single most basic precondition to human existence in
covenant. It says the same thing to say that the source
of the right to life is to be found in the fact that God
summons us into being, for the existence into which
we are called from nothingness is being in covenant.
If I should have freedom this is because there can be
no fellow humanity without my being free to it, or
rather free to, with, and for another. This brings us to
bodily freedoms, and freedom of action, which belong
also intrinsically and indefeasibly to the exercise and
to the very existence of fellow humanity. My body is
not alien to me or to my being with fellow man. God
who created me an embodied soul or an in-souled body

---

15 Paul Tillich, *The Courage to Be* (New Haven: Yale University
Press, 1952), Chs. 4 and 5.

at the same time gave me a nature in the form of fellow humanity in the historical time and space of my existence in covenant. In existing in my body, I have life, I am free, I say Thou and in so doing am I, I am my being with other men. This is the meaning of freedoms of speech and of action.

The same can be said of "private" property or a space in which to live and means by which to live as a right of fellow humanity. This implies, of course, that I need some things to call my own in order to be with or for fellow man. Otherwise, I would be without a place on which to stand with him. He would then be without me, and I without him. I would sink into relations with the state or institutions above me which would absorb us both. There would be no distancing by which I would bring more and more of a self to the bond of covenant between us. There would be less I-ness and Thou-ness, and only between-ness there where we once attempted to stand with one another in mutual address. This is one of the meanings of saying that property as a human right finds its justification, and as well its responsible limits, in the precariousness of fellow humanity in every man, and not in the claims of a human nature that, without fellow man, demands to be supreme above physical things in appropriating them to the direction of its rational will in isolation.

At the same time, property as a natural right means simply that this right belongs to my fellow humanity in the sense that my duty to serve the just cause among men and to destine property to the common good is not an open question for me to decide. The direction of the space or place I occupy on the earth into the time of my covenant with fellow man ought not to be regarded in every respect as only an option to be chosen or not, according as this pleases me or not. This seems especially to be the case with regard to the ownership and use of property for doing business with the public. Such property is mine expressly for the sake of the life of man with man. In owning it, I belong generically to the race of mortal and needy men. The definition of such property right should itself contain an indissoluble and *unavoidable* connection between my ownership and the good of all men who in time come to that spot with needs I have so used my property as to be able to provide for. God, who creates and sustains justice among men, purposes them to live in unbreakable covenant with Him and with all who, like God in Christ, bear the human countenance. As the promise and anticipation, the pre-condition and the external possibility of even minimum yet unbreakable covenant between man and man, the "inn keeper's law" is clearly a rule of law found in the fashion of fellow humanity.

2

"Law and Order" with Charity

Whether the "inn keeper's law" *is* actually in fact our law of public property is not so easily decided as the foundation of this rule in natural justice. The law of the land in this regard is not so readily determined as the morality of the matter. It is not quite certain (as Martin Luther King seemed to me to imply on *Meet the Press*) that the same Supreme Court which decided as it did when it struck down compulsory segregation in public education will also uphold the Negro's *legal* right (his moral right is not at this point the issue) to be served at lunch counters. This may prove true, and we may hope that it will. But that statement obscures a needed distinction between state action in the public schools and the action or rights of individual property owners. From the legal right of any person not to be segregated for reasons of race by the governing body of a community that by state action provides education at public expense, we can conclude only that the same is likely to be also the rule of law in the case of the "wade-ins" at *public* beaches, or in the case of restaurants in *public* buildings, etc.

Now, whether the "wade-ins" are "lawful" in our legal system while the sit-ins may be "unlawful," or whether both are "lawful" as well as just, is a consideration of some importance for Christian social attitudes and action. Of course, in our law any person has the right to take reasonable, and sometimes unreasonable, action *to find out what are his legal rights,* to make himself a test case, calling by such direct action for a decision to be made with regard to him, for the clarification of the legal status of general human rights in his particular case, and then for the enforcement of these rights he believes he should have. Such litigation is an important part of Anglo-American jurisprudence, and of the relation of people to law. In this way, the sit-ins are certainly *legally* justifiable, to provoke the juridical determination of the law, or even an extension or change in existing law by judicial interpretation. Since "we don't have a declaratory Constitution, the question of constitutionality has to be tested."[1] "Are these [city] ordinances or [state] laws constitutional? The conduct might violate the city ordinance but the city ordinance might be unconstitutional, and you frequently have to have a test case. *You have to violate a city ordinance in an orderly fashion,* so to speak, in order that its constitutionality may be tested."[2] Moreover, many of the *arrests* have been clearly *illegal.* "In some instances, the Negroes had left the premises. They were ordered to leave and they left. The police still arrested them. In one case, the policeman testified, when the lawyer asked all the questions about what they were doing, were they dis-

---

[1] Clement Vose, Associate Professor of Government at Wesleyan University, on *The Open Mind:* "The Living Constitution—Civil Rights and the Negro," NBC-TV, December 4, 1960.

[2] J. W. Peltason, Professor of Political Science at the University of Illinois, *The Open Mind,* December 4, 1960, italics added.

orderly, etc., etc., the policeman said no. Then he was asked the question: Assuming that this defendant did exactly the same thing that he did and he had been white, would he have been arrested? And the policeman said: 'Certainly not.' "[3]

Still the importance of asking concerning an action —even one to the good end of changing social relationships in a direction which is firmly believed to be toward greater justice—whether it is "lawful" or "unlawful," legal or illegal, becomes clear if we ask ourselves the hypothetical question: Suppose (God forbid) the Supreme Court were to rule that ours is not the "inn keeper's law"; what then should be a sound judgment for a Christian to make upon a proposal that he join in *direct* action against this law in order to change it, or to alter practices in the community so that a property owner may not do what the law, thus construed, says he has a right to do?

A simple appeal to the Anglo-Saxon common law or to natural justice does not settle the question that has just been raised. Statutory law has, in many areas and for good reason, "repealed" the common law. Moreover, the meaning of the common law for the law of today is always a matter of judicial opinion; and, since American law split off from English law, both based on the common law, it is the courts in America who say what the applicable rules of law drawn from the common law *may mean* in cases in which these rules are held to be decisive. We do not yet know whether our

---

[3] Thurgood Marshall, Special Counsel of the National Association for the Advancement of Colored People, *The Open Mind*, December 4, 1960.

law is the "inn keeper's law," or that local practices and local or state ordinances to the contrary will be struck down by higher courts, or whether the right of private property includes the power to refuse service, until this is tested in the courts. In the recent sit-ins, for example, we as a people may be grateful that in many instances, because this was a bold and non-violent protest movement and because of wise and courageous community leadership and by the action of individual property owners, local customs and the habits of people were changed, sometimes with comparative ease, and that local ordinances which might have enforced a right to refuse service as part of private property right were often not invoked. Still this leaves in doubt what is the rule of law the courts will apply, and it leaves determination of the law in this vital area to the ordinances now on the books, as these may be construed by law enforcement officials and used or not used by them, and to city fathers and state legislators in the laws they may yet enact.

The fact, therefore, that it was hard to know what law should be sought to be applied to the sit-ins and that it was hard for the participants to get a clear test case had also this result: custom and practice have happily been changed in many places but we may not yet know the meaning of the legal rights of property owners in this regard. What these are in our legal system is surely of importance where local custom and the practice of discrimination in restaurants or hotels may not easily crumble, and in face of defensive legislative measures that have been and may yet be enacted. This was by no means determined by the success of the sit-ins in a good many cities. Indeed, by virtue of their success it was not. Were the young people engaged in these demonstrations creating a riot? Likely not they, but those who on occasion attacked them. Were they loitering? Better not press that charge, since store-owners characteristically invite people to loiter on their premises. Were they acting in restraint of trade? Why, they wanted only to expand trade. Were they trespassing? This would seem the charge best calculated to find out what the law is that the courts will uphold.

The fact seems to be that, in some state jurisdictions of the United States, an "inn keeper's law" has been promulgated by legislation defining the terms under which hotels and restaurants will be licensed, prohib-iting them to refuse service; in other states, legislation regulating the licensing of these establishments specifi-cally repeals any "inn keeper's law" there may be in the common law, by prohibiting the service of both whites and Negroes together. The sit-ins in the South have been directed against variety stores which are *not* licensed as restaurants and whose lunch counters no one thought to regulate by more than custom. In some instances, these may still come under the ordinances of certain departments of state government, such as the Health and Welfare Department, prohibiting unsegre-gated service. One result of sit-ins in some states may be that the state legislatures will fill in this lacuna in their laws requiring segregation through the licensing power. Meantime, within the gap left by state licens-ing regulations, there may be cases of arrest for tres-pass (after refusal to leave a counter whose proprietor has exercised the supposed right in his property to refuse service) going forward for resolution in the courts above, which will determine whether, in the absence of explicit state legislation to the contrary, our law of semi-public property is in fact the "inn keeper's law." Clarification of the rule of law to be applied may not be forthcoming from the legal actions set in motion by the sit-ins in Atlanta, which led most unfortunately to the heavy-handed injustice of Martin Luther King's four months' jail sentence for a traffic violation. Apart from the revocation of his suspended sentence for driving without a license, at issue was a *new* Georgia law making it a misdemeanor to refuse to leave private property when requested to do so. This statute clearly repealed any "inn keeper's law" that might, in our unwritten legal tradition, be asserted to be applicable. Unless and until this statute is struck down by a higher court, a property owner has the legal right, in this state jurisdiction, to refuse service at lunch counters. And the owners of these stores refused to prosecute under that statute, and Mayor Hartsfield of Atlanta wanted it understood that King's rearrest and sentencing took place *outside* of the enlightened city of Atlanta.

If the "inn keeper's law" is not our law, if in fact Negroes do not have a legal right to be served at lunch counters and restaurants or to be on other "private" business property just like other kinds of people who are welcomed there and subject to the same regulations that apply to them, then we would have to say that, in the order of charity, such property with all the power this places in the owner should still be destined by him to his life with and for man. Supposing the proprietor to have a *legal* right to serve or not to serve whomever he pleases; then would arise for the Christian the crucial question whether this right, granted him in the legal system, should in charity ever be exercised. The legal system, or even the reality of justice believed to be behind this, or a public policy that attributes to a restaurant or hotel owner the power to decide to give or withhold his services to people as he pleases and according to kinds or races as he wishes, all this grants him only the right and the power to do this. This does not determine whether he should ever exercise this power or right. The Christian who lives also in the order of charity must ask himself not only what legal justice permits but also what love requires him to do. Here, in fact, is a source from which, as charity sovereignty shapes our conceptions of justice and our practices, this may become the law—if in fact it is not now the case that legally a man must not practice racial discrimination in the economic order on which, as an indispensable precondition, fellow humanity so evidently depends.

In the light of the Christian understanding of man's life in institutions and under law, and especially in view of the sinfulness that also enters into any struggle for greater justice in general practice, Christians should have a deep concern to know what *in fact* the law *is* in every decision they make about the direct action it is legitimate to take. We know that, while love transforms justice, as it were, from above, ordinarily the social and legal system is moved from below by pressures, and justice is usually found amid the jar of opposing forces and between contending factions, each of which is quite sure its is the true justice. Here must enter a realistic interpretation of the state and its law as God's governance of a fallen world in which go on all our strivings for greater justice; and the legitimacy of order must be stressed alongside claims for justice. Whether our law *is in fact* the "inn keeper's law" has importance for Christian decision, as well as our reasons for saying that this *should be* the law.

We need not repeat that an owner's having the legal right to refuse service and his exercising it are by no means the same thing. Our question now has to do with Christian participation in action definable as "against the law." Is this, or how is this, a part of Christian responsibility? This issue is often obscured by the use of deliberately unclear language. It would better contribute to this nation's public discussion for a political convention to voice its approval of the sit-ins forthrightly, than by only seeming to do so under the rubric of supporting the right of assemblage for "peaceful protest." This circumlocution begs the question that needs to be kept clear in a nation under law, since an assemblage for peaceful protest has no legal right to take place on private property against its owner's wishes, but only outside on the streets or in public parks, etc. It has to be assumed that such persons have a legal right to be there for the more primary purpose of being served food, or that they are there to test what their rights are, before it can be argued that they are, at the lunch counters, exercising a right of peaceful protest against a denial of their rights.

So far—as is proper first—we have spoken of the Christian understanding of man's life in political, legal and economic community in its positive aspect. Christians also know, however, a darker side to our human reality and a negative, or restraining, purpose of God in justice and law. Sin croucheth at the door of man's life with his fellow man. Created for life in covenant-community, man has always already broken this covenant for which he was made in his fellow humanity. Because Christians know man not only in the light but also in the shadow cast by the light of Jesus Christ *the* man *for* other men, they acknowledge how far short every human relationship comes from being life *for* fellow man, and consequently they discern, perhaps more clearly than otherwise they would see to be the case, how far short every relation in life comes from being life *with* fellow man.

We recognize man's propensity not only to be neutral or without his fellow man, but to stand in relation to him only for oneself. This means that the achievement of more abundant expressions of fellow humanity in the social order generally, no less and even more than in marriage, needs the "garments of skin" (Gen. 3:21) with which God by his own hands clothed naked human relations. This is a symbol for God's restraining grace in every impersonal and co-ercive institution and in the legal order, by which he intends for our good always to preserve a tolerable fellow humanity against the ravagements of sin. This is the justification for Christian realism in support of law and the established order unless and until some better garment can be woven without letting worse befall. Doubtless these orders partake of the sin and injustice they repress. But in the Christian view, simple and not so simple injustice *alone* has never been a sufficient justification for revolutionary change. There is always also the question of order to be considered, and a need for restraints placed upon all and upon the injustice infecting even our claims for greater justice. The Christian stands, then, for the rule of law against every utopian liberalism, however highminded; and, fortunately, an understanding of the need for law and order as well as for greater justice still have powerful influence in American political life. However, in the world at large, there is abundant evidence that utopian expectations lead to government from the streets and to charismatic leaders ruling by force because they are believed to incarnate, and do incarnate, a people's unlimited and un-self-critical craving for justice.

Christian action aims, of course, to transform the social order, to improve the administration of justice, to obtain justice for all based on a genuine relation of man *with* man, or even to refashion that justice more and more in the direction of man *for* fellow man, and to show mercy not only through the interstitial spaces of the social system but, as far as possible, throughout the system itself as well. In all this, quite properly the Christian should aim *ahead* of the flying bird of justice in order actually just to strike it. But he does not shoot into another dimension, or aim at pure I-Thou-ness without limiting and clothing garments. He does not expect justice without law, nor fellow humanity without impersonal ways of keeping that from becoming man against man in the best of causes. He knows that man with and for fellow man is the goal toward which we are being redeemed; but precisely because this in its fulness is the ethics of redemption, he knows that it is not here but in the eschatological event toward which God's covenant moves. In his response to God the Redeemer and God the Creator of our fellow creatureliness, he does not omit to respond obediently also to God's judgment, by being content to live within orders that limit and often obscure while they still make possible man's life in community and hold this back from death and destruction.

Especially when, in the political order, an effort is made to achieve the natural rights of fellow humanity and to define these as civil or legal rights, the Christian remembers what has just been said concerning law, institutions, and the socio-political order as a garment of skin by which alone the justice of man with man may be protected and sin restrained. The distance between man and man has to be *increased* in a fallen world, in contrast to the created ordering which human existence may have had in the Garden of Paradise, precisely in order to preserve in extant social orders the possibility and the promise of covenant, precisely in order that man's life with fellow man may not perish from the earth. For example, the positive reason why all citizens should without discrimination have the right to vote, full participation in the discussion of public policy, and eligibility for leadership or for office, is because this is a requirement of the fellow humanity that belongs to each and every one with his fellow man, or it is because the state is to be understood as an organized covenant and a body composed of covenant relations. Yet there is this additional, and negative though no less important, reason for the human right to share in the shaping of policy for the common good, namely, that, as Lincoln said, no man is good enough to rule another without his consent.

Similarly, it should not be supposed thoughtlessly that the less that privacy and the protective role of civil rights are stressed, the better; or that the more justice is emphasized as man's life in community with his fellow man, and the more energetically we seek directly to transform this justice by mercy, the better. Mankind by now should have learned the political wisdom of which Christians are placed on notice by what they are given to know about repeatedly broken covenants. To soften institutions and do away with impersonal relations and level a king's highway for men to venture forth toward life with their fellows also at the same time removes obstacles that may be needed to prevent universally sinful men from taking the castle where dwells in everyone his life. This can destroy (as surely as when man is regarded as a creature in isolation) the presuppositions and external basis of covenant and man's capability for his life with fellow man. This is one reason it will never cease to be necessary in any good covenant community for men to have the right to things that they own, even if it is most certainly true that a legitimate right to private property, if it belongs to man, belongs to man in the form of fellow humanity, or to him in order that he may the better be with his neighbor.

The Neighborhood School and Planned Integration

Here a disturbing example may be given. Abstract notions of equality and resort to law and radical changes in public institutions, for the purpose of allowing people to be with and for others, may only shatter the natural communities on which any social order must rest that has not been reduced to relating individuals to one another unit-wise under an unlimited mass democracy. I refer to the way in which the Supreme Court's invalidation of enforced segregation in public schools along racial lines has been interpreted as requiring enforced desegregation (a step that was certainly necessary) and then, in New York City and elsewhere, as enforced integration without regard for neighborhood. After two years of controversy and under great pressure from "understandably impatient" groups threatening a "sit-out" and demanding for their children their "right to an integrated education," the New York City Board of Education on Sept. 1, 1960 announced a plan for "open registration" or "permissive zoning." A *New York Times* editorial in approval of this plan stated that "it reverses long-standing policy, based on the ideal of the neighborhood school, and on the argument that residential segregation, while a fact in most of the municipal area, must be solved on the level of housing rather than of education." This was a large concession in principle to those groups who "look rather to the schools as the spearhead toward an integrated community." This editorial concluded on a futuristic note in order to justify any such thing as sound public policy: "The ultimate hope is, of course, that some day the Board of Education's original and sound ideal of neighborhood schools will return to a city of harmonious integrated neighborhoods"—when in short the schools can cease to be used as an instrument for total social reform and can be returned to their function of providing education for the children of a community.

The plan itself was modest enough. The first year it applied only to students *entering* the first year of junior high or high school, and a select list of such schools were designated as "sending" or as "receiving" schools. Three thousand were expected to apply; and then in September, 1961, some form of "open registration" will be applied to elementary schools. It was estimated that only about 15,000 students in years to come would elect to go to schools outside their districts. It should be said that the high schools of the city already enroll from wide areas; and that, because of distinctions in the kind of education each provides, there is little neighborhood zoning on this level. On the other side, it should be pointed out that the same result could have been achieved on grounds other than a total social policy of integrating the races (in contrast to a policy of desegregating the schools), since the "sending" schools are now overcrowded and the "receiving" schools under-utilized. Also it was recognized that to forestall mass exodus these "sending" schools would have to be rapidly improved, and that the "receiving" schools would have to expand their remedial reading programs which before may have been rightly concentrated in schools in neighborhoods where the Puerto Rican children had special need for this.

The point here is not the details of the plan, but whether there is a better principle of order to be found than that of the neighborhood school when from this has been stricken any registration of pupils *by the schools* along racial lines or any gerrymandering in zoning; and whether in fact a positive policy of undertaking to provide an integrated education for all children, standing alone in abstraction from other facets of community life, is an ordering principle at all. It is noteworthy that public officials and spokesmen for all sorts of civic and service organizations voiced approval of this plan—all except the president of the Parents' Workshop for Equity in New York City Schools, which spearheaded the attack on the idea of neighborhood schools and threatened "sit-outs" unless the Board announced "a plan and timetable for school desegregation and immediate transfer for those children whose parents want an integrated education." The argument was that token "open registration," without buses provided, offers "no immediate help to 122,000 minority group families"; and this may be quite correct if a "right to an integrated education" guaranteed by the state has now descended upon the heads of each and every child no matter where he lives.

It is clear that if order results from such notions of abstract justice, removing the fabric of community between man and man, and not disorder, it will be because the idea of a neighborhood school continues to operate in the preference of a majority of parents. It will be because only a limited number of them petition for the removal of their children from schools in districts that are predominantly Negro or Puerto Rican in population. If the "right to an integrated education" (in contrast to the right not to be forcefully segregated by the public school system itself) is made an absolute, then the only way to insure this and prevent an absolute decline of schools in districts that are predominantly of one race would be to use the children of the minority white population of Manhattan as pawns "sent" into the schools of various localities, forcefully integrating everyone in order that anyone may have his right to an integrated education. Having abandoned the neighborhood school as a sound principle regulating school attendance, the Board of Education will find no other clear ground to stand on. To avoid *unintentional* segregation, the school board's policy would have to become *intentional* integration, i.e., enrollment *along racial lines,* but this time by mixing the pupils according to race. This would be an ironic conclusion to which to come in practice. Yet something like this is bound to be the result of attending only to abstract equality and togetherness in our policy-making, and of forgetting the distance between man and man and the fabric of real community which public institutions ought to rest upon and not destroy.[4]

---

[4] For the above, see *The New York Times* of September 1, 2, 3, and 7, 1960. On September 21 the *Times* reported that only 397 students out of an expected 3,000 applied to be transferred from junior high schools; and on October 13 that less than 4 per cent of eligible elementary school pupils applied. The latter news story commented that "Negroes and Puerto Ricans apparently want the right to send their children to schools in other areas, even though they do not necessarily want to send them." It is understandable that a people coming out of the Egypt of their bondage to enforced discriminatory practices should want this. But an "interim ethic" for them is hardly a sound basis for public or educational policy.

The Board of Education later announced that it plans in 1961-62 to provide transportation for elementary pupils whose parents wish to transfer them to more multi-racial schools (*Times,* Dec. 3, 1960). Also, the Board plans to extend integration next year by enlarging

Integration and the Familial Quality in Churches

The church itself, as an actual community and social institution, may be taken as a second illustration of the need for really cohesive relationships among people— relations that have concrete significance for them— rather than idealized assertions of community or abstract constitutions for togetherness. Kyle Haselden

---

the "reserve" of newly eligible pupils in an attempt to secure as many as 2,500 Negro and Puerto Rican transferees. According to the New York *Herald Tribune,* Jan. 13, 1961, this is "regarded as a hedge against a repeat of the board's experience last fall, when only 397 of 12,000 eligible pupils applied for 3,000 openings."

The use of school funds to insure integrated education for pupils (as distinct from avoiding state action that segregates them) is a questionable banner to unfurl before the nation in this historical moment when many parents in the South would like to have tax assistance in transporting their children also away from their present school districts where, if as yet only token, desegregation has been achieved (as distinct from integration along racial lines). This can only confirm their suspicions that the public schools are planned to be used as a direct instrument for social change and not for the education of *all alike without discrimination.*

The suit recently brought to determine whether there is segregation by gerrymandering or other means in the school districts of New Rochelle, New York, is, of course, a perfectly proper and necessary action to insure that the public schools, not only in the South, are not themselves being used as an instrument of segregation. For a long time to come, the courts will have to review the actions of local school boards; and the Supreme Court may have to serve as a "National School Board" in the sense that it will insure against denial of rights by local public officials. (It is odd that Protestant liberals who hold this obviously correct opinion with regard to legal protection against denial of rights to non-white children often protest against making the Court a National School Board in the matter of prohibiting the promotion of religion in the public schools.) In the proper exercise of their function, the courts should, of course, carefully scrutinize the policies of local school boards. In enforcing the law against compulsory segregation perhaps it is now time for the courts to direct every school board to show good faith in desegregation. At least, the burden should be taken off the plaintiffs in assuring that the law of the land is observed. This, coupled with the stair-step or grade-a-year plan of desegregation, leads to the result that "the students who file the lawsuit never get their benefits. They are school children when they file the suit, and then we have this interesting anomaly in the law—of a court's saying that your constitutional rights are satisfied by somebody else's getting his" (Thurgood Marshall, *The Open Mind,* December 4, 1960).

has written a most extraordinary and penetrating book on the subject of race relations.[5] He achieves a unique interweaving of Christian and social science perspectives upon this problem; and his analysis stands head and shoulders above all other attempts to deal with morality and race relations from a Christian point of view. Yet the reader will feel that Haselden begins to lean on his oars a bit when he comes directly to that human community he knows best: the churches.

Before taking up the theme, "Toward a Racially United Church," this author had comprehended the ethical issues in race relations generally under the rubric of "what all men owe to all men." This is our order of creation or natural justice. He had comprehended the special Christian perspective in race relations in these terms: "what the Christian owes to all men." This is justice inspired, elevated, and transformed by Christian love. Finally he steps over into the sphere of the church, which he calls "what the Christian owes to the Christian." Here also, of course, it is clear what ideally should be the case.

For no matter what the churches are sociologically, theirs should be a "oneness which men have in Christ, not 'after the flesh' but 'after the spirit,' not in the solid and shared flesh of men but in the broken and shared body of Christ. . . ."[6] This means that "the question as to whether or not a Negro should be admitted into the fellowship of other Christians should not even be debatable; if he applies as a Christian he

---

[5] *The Racial Problem in Christian Perspective* (New York: Harper & Brothers, 1959).

[6] *Ibid.,* p. 189.

does not apply as a Negro." To debate this would be for the community to surrender its right to the appellation *Christian*.[7] Finally, Haselden condemns as a "strange and disturbing development" the practice of accepting as equals in the white Protestant church only Negroes who "first qualify socially or professionally." In that case a Negro "ceases to be the excluded 'Jew' only by becoming the acceptable 'Greek.' " However, the church should rest on none of those standards or distinctions. It rests rather upon its foundation in the fact that, while "in the creation, God said 'Let there be male and female '; spiritually, in Christ, God said, 'Let there be neither male nor female,' " etc.[8] This means that "the ancient scoffer's description of Christianity as 'sexless, homeless, nationless' [and, may we not add, colorless, ethnically rootless, *déclassé*, educationless, etc.?] is a figurative yet precise description of what the Christian community should be."[9]

Therefore divisive differences of any sort, when measured against the *idea* and the *reality* of the church, can remain only as *phantasms* of deluded minds and prejudiced hearts. "Where the Christian sees his fellow Christian as anything other than a Christian, he has called forth a *specter* which has its embodiment only in his own mind and heart, an *apparition* which fades and disappears as he himself is lost in Christ."[10] Yet the nth conclusion to be reached by this movement of thought is quite questionable.

---

[7] *Ibid.*, p. 191. Haselden adds: "This, of course, is to speak ideally about the matter."

[8] *Ibid.*, p. 293.

[9] *Ibid.*, pp. 293-4.

[10] *Ibid.*, p. 194 (italics added).

The fact is that anyone who saw only such Christians around him on Sunday morning would be seeing specters. He could not see his wife and children, but only some nondescript creatures in their stead, to be denotated *Christians as such* but with little connotation besides. He would be homeless and community-less, which means that the man of flesh and blood he really is would fade and disappear away, lost in Christ.

It may be seriously questioned whether Christ came to save such apparitions, and not men and women who still share solidly in the flesh while they live out of the broken and shared body of Christ and live by the Spirit toward the event of the final transformation of this life into the kingdom of Christ. Of course, in the sphere of the church the tension ought to be greatest between what men are and what they are to become. In the church the saving distinction ought to be kept clear between nature and grace, between creation and covenant, between the cohesions of any actual human community and the fact that we are and therefore are to become one in Christ. Among the people of God there should be the greatest possible openness to have the community we now have transformed into the community that may and will be. No let or hindrance should be placed upon Christian love's elevating the justices of men, and especially the church that now is, to a higher and more perfect power.

Still, it is clear that regulative ideal Christian descriptions of perfect community sought to be made constitutive of the actual historical human community of the church may prove as disruptive as can merely abstract notions of justice in society generally, when these are sought to be applied without a proper regard for order, for neighborhood, and for affinities that constitute this humanity of ours during this time between the times. This is to deny neither the reality of the church and the oneness among Christians as these are described in the New Testament, nor the continual transforming impact this ideal reality should have upon our actual church community. Especially in the church there should be a permanent revolution going on.

But with regard to every one of those statements it ought also to be remembered that the Spirit and the church He creates are eschatological realities; and that, while oneness is rightly said to be the life of every Christian with and for his fellow Christian, this life is also declared to be hid with Christ in God (Col. 3:3). The reality of community in Christ is far from irrelevant to action in the present time, in church and in society. This is the lure and the guide and the power for our present action. But the realization of perfect community in Christ is not separated from us now by only the "long run," or by distance in time from this goal. To the end of time, community in Christ will remain a *judgmental* standard, calling for radical criticism of any actual church or any actual society. This we mean by saying the church is now militant, not triumphant; and that in this age Christ's kingship is known by faith and not by sight.

Eschatological realities sought to be made directly constitutive of this our life, as well as the justice that exhibits the pure creation which was in the Garden of Paradise, may be so apprehended as to lead to quite inadequate response on the part of living men to God's creative, judging, preserving, and redeeming power in the world or in the church. People may find that they have abstracted themselves from this world and from these churches, and vainly imagined that they are some other sort of men than they really are and that as such they are called to obey God in some other sort of world. When this happens it will be found that we have lost the capacity to be undergoing change by creation-covenant in which and toward which we live and by the ultimate reality of the church and the Spirit of Christ. For the persons we also really are and the communities we also really have with fellow men and with fellow Christians will have faded in their significance for us and disappeared in the best of causes, "lost in Christ."

Therefore in realistic acknowledgement of the components of church community, it seems to me, Haselden applies the brakes somewhat in analyzing the preconditions for a racially united church. It is true, of course, that there is racial snobbery and spiritual isolation to be overcome. It is true that there are racially segregating as well as racially separated churches. It is true that "the white man made and keeps the Negro church a necessity of wholesome Negro life."[11] These things ought not to be. Still, "the factors buttressing exclusiveness in the white Protestant churches are components of the Protestant concept of the nature of the church." These components are: voluntariness of church membership; the complete freedom of the in-

---

[11] *Ibid.*, p. 198.

dividual to attend the church of his choice rather than the church appointed for his geographical area; the democratic and representative character of church government; the social and familial functions of the church; a sense of solidarity as a requisite of church life; the church as *koinonia* rather than *ekklesia,* and the freedom of the churches from episcopal edict which more readily can achieve a less worthwhile integration. All these things are "permissive of racial division rather than racially divisive."[12] Those things are not about to be given up for the sake of some less personal and less social surrogate for oneness in Christ. ". . . The temptation will be," Haselden writes, "for Protestants to forego their familial quality and social functions so that Negroes may be accepted into membership without offense to the prejudiced."[13]

Now, how on this earth are the Protestant churches, both white and Negro, "to preserve their stress upon the role of the church as a family of Christians who are in covenant with one another and with God, and at the same time to welcome into all the social associations of such a fellowship all who profess Christ as Lord and Saviour, irrespective of their race or social status?"[14] In answer to this question there seems to be a suggestion growing out of the fact that the Negro churches (which are separate and not separatist churches) "multiplied their functions in Negro life." They "soon became for their people the primary, indeed the sole, social unit"; "a voice of protest and of

[12] *Ibid.,* pp. 195-213.
[13] *Ibid.,* p. 213.
[14] *Ibid.*

hope; a training ground for [the Negro's] developing
leadership"; and "a leverage for political and economic
and social advancement."[15] This suggestion also grows
out of the fact that only somewhat less have white
Protestant churches been the centers of community
life in this country.

It is a surprisingly conservative conclusion (not
therefore necessarily incorrect) with regard to church
community, which this author knows best and esteems.
"The racially separated churches will therefore disappear only as the total social and religious climate
that now naturally sustains them is replaced by a climate in which they can exist only as forced and arti-
ficial social structures."[16] One aspect of the requisite
"climatic" changes that should have first to take place
may be singled out. This is that the Negro become "so
thoroughly absorbed into the various forms of national
life that the racial church serves no longer as the primary 'social cosmos' of Negro life."[17] If white churches
served any longer as the center of community life, the
same "development" would, presumably, have to take
place in them. The climatic changes would seem to require the Negro churches to become about as unimportant for large ranges of the actual lives of men
and women as have our bourgeois white churches!
Then will the end come—the end to divided, volun-
taristic, and still familial churches. In any case, there
will have to be decisive changes in the Negro church,
the white man's church, the white man's state, and the

---

15 *Ibid.,* p. 201-2.
16 *Ibid.,* p. 214.
17 *Ibid.,* p. 215.

white man's society before "all areas of Christian community" will "be opened to all members of the Christian family," and not merely "the mutual occupation
of a common space, the joining of voices in worship
and prayer," and "the sharing of a hymnal."[18] Is this
not rather like the futuristic note in the *Times'* editorial, pointing to a time beyond the present time of
man's life with man when there can be a return to
the sound ideal of neighborhood schools—when there
can be real oneness in Christ along with real oneness
in the fabric of actual community life in all its concrete and personal aspects? The Christian, indeed,
must point to such a time; but in referring to the kingdom of Christ which is not of this world as the power
and the guidance for human life and for the empirical
life of the churches, he should make sure that he does
this as a man fully involved in this world and its communities, and not abstracted from them. It is within
the solid and shared flesh of men and within the
divided flesh of mankind that we partake of the broken
and shared body of Christ, or not at all. It is to men
and women, who are always male and female, that it is
said that in Christ there is neither male or female, or
this is said to no one. It is as white or Negro, educated
or uneducated, Jew or Greek, etc., who have never seen
a *Christian as such* that men enact and participate in
covenant with God and with fellow man, or else there
is no covenant and no transforming influence of Christian love within the actualities of real human history
—in or, for that matter, outside the churches. This is

18 *Ibid.*, pp. 212-13.

the world and the churches upon which the *judg-mental* standard of community in Christ can and may and must have transforming impact. This provides, to the end of time, regulative critical criteria and ulti-mate guidance and power for human conduct and for right relations of man with and for his fellow man.

State Action and the Protective Role of Private Property

A third and final illustration of the fact that, espe-cially in the legal and social order, a limit must be placed upon the means used to advance the cause of justice, will show that the service of property is to hold people apart from one another and from government as well as to relate them responsibly. The laws of some states now extend the concept of "state action" to in-clude under government the activities of realtors; and with this goes equality before the law in buying and selling houses guaranteed by enforcement, just as the same equality was quite properly applied in the case of state action in public education to prohibit segre-gation. One need not oppose the step taken by these state laws, as a means of obtaining greater justice in private housing, in order to notice with some misgiving the fact that the bridge used to extend the concept of "state action" was the "licensing power" of the state; and secondly to notice that not only realtors must apply for their special licenses, but also every house-holder and any man who has ever lived must also have licenses of many sorts, building permits, etc., from state and local governments; and to conclude from this that if state action, without some sound distinctions in this concept, goes wherever licenses go, then the full force of the state is wherever we are, and fellow humanity is as much endangered as before.

Moreover, the attempt to secure the high goal of greater justice and fellow humanity in the relationships among people in a community by using the state's licensing power to compel realtors to sell property to anyone with the ability to pay may only fall below this goal and establish a cash nexus alone as the relationship pertaining between man and man. Christians have as many, if different, reasons as do the Marxists for fearing that an abstract, arithmetical equality, when this is made the one principle of social cohesion, may lead to worse rather than better results. There are still tendencies in the bourgeois mentality expressed in its best social philosophy and proposals for legal reform that were aptly expressed by Karl Marx:

> There came a time when everything that men had considered inalienable became an object of exchange, of traffic, and could be alienated. This is a time when the very things which till then had been communicated but never exchanged, given but never sold, acquired but never bought—virtue, love, conviction, knowledge, conscience, etc.—when everything passed into commerce. It is the time of general corruption, of universal venality, or, to speak in terms of political economy, the time when everything, moral or physical, having become a marketable value, is brought to the market to be assessed at its truest value . . .; [when are] dissolved all natural organic relationships into money relationships . . .; [putting] an end to all feudal, patriarchial idyllic relations. It has pitilessly torn asunder the motley feudal ties that bound man to his "natural superiors" [and, a Christian would add, underneath these,

all the better covenant relationships as well], and has left no other nexus between man and man than naked self-interest, and callous "cash payment."[19]

It is not immediately obvious that the ability to pay is a better reason for living in a certain neighborhood than other reasons for choosing to do so, if there were any way the latter could be freely and fairly exercised by buyer and seller and neighbors alike. Taking into account the warning these words can be seen to contain as to the probably vast difference between the community we are aiming at by law and the community we are going to achieve, we may still be compelled to conclude that on balance this risk has to be ventured, since only the *external* basis for covenant or the *possibility* of greater fellow humanity is all the social order can achieve in any case.

In general, the stress ought not be too heavily placed on the protective role of property, or on the distances there must be between man and man in the fabric of community life. It is true that in the days of an ascendant individualism, a man was in danger of being without fellow man; while today and in the future— always, of course, in the name of progress and greater justice—his fellow man may be in danger of being without him, or both without each other, each having disappeared from the place that sustained him into relations without distance. Still equal or greater weight should be given to the need for *unavoidable* if impersonal connections, preserved by law, between man and man. The task of statesmanship in effecting a solu-

---

[19] *The Communist Manifesto.*

tion of the problem posed by segregation in residential housing is to insure that the sparse dwelling places on this earth are not monopolized by the same kind or race of people who came first to occupy and own them, even if this results in some disruption of existing natural affinities among people. The law can at best insure in impersonal ways that there is minimal evidence of man's co-humanity with every man as only an external sign of his created destiny for community. Just as there is human need for the garment of property in its protective, more personal forms; so also a garment of thick skin is necessary to preserve in many impersonal forms of property, and by arrangements to insure the right to purchase without discrimination, some unavoidable potential connection of every man with his fellow man. This is why we have said that the "inn keeper's law" has its basis in natural justice. Both the manifestation and the limits upon the right of property are for the sake of fellow humanity, since man was not created to be alone; and both persons in covenant must have places on which to stand in the economic and political order for them ever to give substance to the relatedness of man with man.

We have spoken of the danger there may be in an unlimited extension of the concept of state action through the licensing power of the state. It ought not thoughtlessly to be supposed that, simply because we are certain what the membership policies of a private tennis club should be, there would be clear gain for the cause of justice if we as a nation become willing to search for any possible means (building permits, zoning regulations, etc.) to connect its policy up with

state action and thus to force it to do what it should.
It is well to remember that one of the devices used in
the attempt to break the Montgomery Bus Boycot was
an injunction against the car-pools operated by the
Negroes because these were private enterprises operat-
ing *without license fee or franchise.* This injunction
went into force on the day (Nov. 13, 1956) the Supreme Court delivered its verdict upholding a lower
court decision that segregation in public transportation is unconstitutional; and a decision was never
reached on the legal merits of action to upset the injunction, nor on the arrest of Negroes on the charge
that they were conspiring to restrain the normal operation of a business.[20] In order to succeed, protestors on
behalf of greater justice need to have preserved for
them ground on which to stand, where they are free
of state dictation; and this is also the ground or sphere
of freedom their opponents often use to mount a
defense against them!

The same may be the case if the difference between
tax-support and tax-exemption is allowed to collapse;
or if additional steps are taken in the direction of declaring that, while property holders still *have* certain
rights of contract with their property, the state will no
longer *enforce* such rights. It has been suggested that
this last distinction may be the legal resolution in cases
arising out of the sit-ins, i.e., that instead of appealing
to the common law principle governing an inn keeper
the courts will apply the 1948 rule of law in the "re-

---

[20] Martin Luther King, *Stride toward Freedom* (New York:
Harper & Brothers, 1958), pp. 159-60, 183.

strictive covenants" cases to stores that refuse service to Negroes on the grounds that stores are private property. This means that the courts may declare that an owner *has* the right to refuse service, and even to do this in a discriminatory way and himself to evict anyone from his store; but that when he invokes law enforcement agencies to protect him in this right this then becomes a matter of "state action" that may not be used to enforce segregation.[21]

In the opinion of the present writer, the idea that a man *possesses* certain rights which he may not have *enforced* and protected in the civil order is, indeed, a very odd idea. It leads to the notion that he has rights

---

[21] Professor Thomas Emerson of the Yale Law School was ambiguous on this point when he predicted that the Supreme Court may soon sustain the following proposition: "The application of state police force and state judicial systems to prosecuting persons for trespass when they enter a dime store and are asked to leave constitutes discriminatory action and that therefore to that extent the trespass laws are unconstitutional." On the one hand, that statement seems to say that policemen are not private and that any use of them, and of the courts, to enforce laws against trespass in these cases would constitute discriminatory state action (leave standing the laws defining trespass and property rights); while on the other hand, it is clear that in making this statement Mr. Emerson meant to make a sort of appeal to the "inn keeper's law," in order to state his view that such trespass laws were themselves unconstitutional and not only because or at the point at which state action is invoked to enforce them. For he went on to say: "I do not think that the use of police force to expel a person who is not wanted from private property in the sense of a house would be contrary to the Fourteenth Amendment. I also think that a private club, say the West Side Tennis Club, in so far as it is a private tennis club, has a right to choose its own members and that if someone it doesn't want to admit comes into the club to play tennis it can use the police to exclude them. But I think the line must be drawn at those points where the action is in a more public area and I think coming into a store which purports to open its facilities to all people except at the lunch counter is such a proposition" (*The Open Mind*, December 4, 1960). Clearly such a ruling would be a more expansive reading of the rights of individuals among the public invited to be served and a more restrictive reading of the rights of owners of such property. It would not rest upon a refusal of the state to enforce rights left standing in principle.

in some "state of nature" and that more and more of the rights that he has are in fact his only in this mythical state of nature, as civil rights said not to be denied him are yet not legally enforceable. The development of our rules of law in this direction (and the present suggestion indicates how a legal rule introduced in one case tends to become a precedent applicable in other types of cases as well) could lead to the view that while a man *has* freedom to voice some socially objectionable viewpoint in public parks, the law will not protect him in the exercise of this right against the arbitrary action of town councils or against mob action; or that while men *have* freedom of religion they may not call for state action to guarantee them this right if the religion is objected to by the conscience of a vast majority of the citizens or is otherwise against public policy (say, if there were a voluntary religious organization determined to admit people of one race only). Of course, any civil right has to be limited, by other rights and by the rights of others, and by common judgments of morality in extreme instances (e.g., Mormon polygamy). But would it not be better if this were done forthrightly—by legislation, or by the courts' declaring that the right in question entails no such freedom as was sought to be exercised, rather than by means of a subtle distinction between the meaning of the rights men have and those aspects of the exercise of these rights that are not enforceable in the courts and by state action? Commenting upon the fact that lawyers for the sit-in participants are contending, "among other things, that even if a private store has a right to exclude Negroes, enforcement of that attitude by the police makes it official and unconstitutional," Mr. Anthony Lewis, legal reporter for the *New York Times,* correctly analysed the issue: "The trouble is," he wrote, "that if police enforcement is enough to turn private into official discrimination, then the private right has been effectively eliminated." He implied that it would be better if the Court avoided extending that doctrine and instead (as in the recent bus terminal case) gave a more expansive reading to a statute, or a more limiting and responsible reading of the rights of property.[22]

Christian thought and action, therefore, rest not only on a concept of justice but also upon a note of realism about the need for the protection of privacy and of "lesser corporations" as well as for unavoidable fellow humanity in our society. From this point of view, we can only view with some alarm announcements of the goal of complete integration throughout the community life of this nation when this call is sent forth by politicians, in appeal for votes, who *as such* may have no business mixing in the whole community's life, which rather needs to retain a certain degree of independence of the state. Indeed, probing more deeply, we may call attention to a danger in the secular political philosophy behind urgent current attempts to define our "national purpose." A people's purpose is simply together to be a people, to live in political covenant with one another, even as marriage consists of dwelling in covenant. There can be no higher purposes than this, than the enactment and re-enactment

---

[22] *The New York Times,* December 11, 1960.

in time of our fellow humanity. The good life for
men on this earth consists of their life in fidelity with
and for man; this does not first become good when it is
directed toward or subordinated to other ends or objectives, however important some secondary determination of the latter may be. St. Augustine was, therefore, somewhat mistaken in his emphasis when he defined *res publica* as "an assemblage of reasonable beings
bound together by a common agreement as to the objects of their love, . . . whatever it loves,"[23] or as "the
combination of man's wills to attain the things which
are helpful to this life." People do not first agree as to
the objects of their loves, or concerning the things
which will actually prove helpful in this life, or concerning national objectives and goals, and then become a people. The agreement which constitutes *res
publica* is an agreement in willing to be a people; it is
the coming into existence of a covenant community;
and life in covenant means life with and for fellow
man, not life *with* him *for* other objectives. The state
is founded upon no marriage of convenience, however
noble the objectives are supposed to be. Questions
about justice are, therefore, always questions about the
form of a people's will to be a people, whether, and
in what areas for example, the possibility of the practice of segregation violates fundamental political community and contradicts our agreement of wills to be
a people (not whether this practice frustrates our common attainments of *other* goals), and whether this same
life of man with man does not also uphold for man

---

[23] *City of God*, XIX, 24.

an area of freedom to covenant, and consequently a right to privacy, to self-determination in lesser groups, requiring that distance as well as relatedness be externally provided between man and man.

This we say not only because in our fallen world there needs to be distance maintained between man and man, and protective restraints and remedies guaranteed the individual and his voluntary associations even against political encroachment by the champions of greater justice who, we Christians know since we are among them, always share in the sinfulness sought in another of its forms to be repressed by law. This we say also because in the divinely created order, even before sin enters in, for the sake of fellow humanity and in the relatedness of man with man there needs to be distance as well as community, and men have to be free to be with fellow man. Because this is true the social and legal system should provide them with an external basis also for these preconditions of covenant. These conclusions can be reached in Christian social theory without denying that the social and legal order has also the task of assuring for all men the promise and the possibility and often the necessity by law of standing, with all their rights, in positive connection with their fellow man. We are far from saying, therefore, that morality can in no sense be legislated. The foregoing simply states the several factors (among them, liberty), in addition to equality and fraternity, which have to be taken into account in trying to attain the greater justice of man with man in institutions and by law. We say only that the claims of a unitive justice should not thoughtlessly be supposed always to override salutary distinctions in our law that serve the purpose of putting a distance between people and encouraging the growth of all sorts of groups in between government and people in the mass. Then it should be added that, in a fallen world, the claims of justice ought not to override entirely the question of law and order.

The Law and Civil Disobedience

The foregoing, then, are some of the positive and negative reasons why the observance of law is of great importance for Christian thought and practice. Coming directly to this issue, it needs first to be said—and remembered in all that follows—that *precisely because* order and the observance of law is fundamental along with justice, this nation must move rapidly, or with all deliberate *speed,* to achieve a far greater measure of justice in the common life, and especially in race relations. Not only does love create justice, but also justice creates that love or agreement of wills which constitutes a people and differentiates a nation from a mere multitude (Augustine). Such agreement of wills to share in the common life and observe the procedures by which a people rules itself in orderly fashion and gives itself government and laws, these things depend on justice shared by all to the exclusion of none. Wherever there is in our legal system any inbuilt unfairness, there is an open invitation to disorder, especially if blockage becomes apparent in the ways we have established for removing such unfairness and changing law to accord with greater justice. Greater evidence in our laws that this nation is founded upon the recognition of fellow humanity is, therefore, absolutely prerequisite to the preservation for long of the habit of law observance on the part of our people, and for respect for the established procedures by which law grows or is changed.

It is therefore not an indictment of any particular group, least of all those who have suffered and suffer injustice and denial of their rights, but of us all, to say that in American Protestant Christianity (especially in our most stirring pronouncements) we seem often to have had too sentimental a view of advancing the cause of justice and too little concern to probe deeply into the meaning and the theological ethical justification of legality and order. We may not have taken seriously enough, in obedience to God's governance and judgment of a sinful world, our Christian responsibility also to articulate our thinking and discipline our action so as to preserve this world and not some other, and to preserve an orderly, even if unjust, social or legal system while we engage in the struggle for justice within it. This, too, is needed to maintain the fabric of man's life with fellow man, or a garment for covenant. It is well to remember that the Montgomery Bus Boycott was a *refusal* to ride buses on a segregated basis and not direct disobedience to unjust regulations upon boarding them; that a ruling by the courts was sought on whether segregation in public transportation was constitutional or not; that simultaneously earnest attempts were made to find a solution that could be accepted with dignity *within* local and state laws that were being challenged; that arrests for conspiracy to prevent the operation of a lawful business, the injunction against the operation of car pools without a license, and petitions against police harassment never came to decisive legal resolution; and that the bus boycott was victorious because of the moral strength of the people who engaged in this form of public protest *and* because of a Supreme Court decision in their favor interpreting the law of the land. This was not only non-violent resistance against existing "law." It was also responsible resistance in that it was predicated upon the need for obedience to law.

The latter at least as much as the special techniques of resistance that were adopted made this a form of Christian action. Observance of law can be generalized as a Christian principle, although not the only principle, at least as far as, if not further than, non-violence can be generalized as a way of effecting greatly needed social change. It might even be said that violent means to achieve the same ends (on the supposition also that this could be effective) are to be rejected not chiefly because they are violent but because, as such, they *cannot* be used along with proper respect for the rule of law or while seeking *legally* to change the law and to find out what is the law to be applied in a test case. Public protest movements and direct action must, on the Christian understanding not only of justice remedying sin but of order restraining it, be kept compatible with maintaining the rule of law. Phrases like "non-co-operation with evil," or the "struggle between justice and injustice, between the forces of light and the forces of darkness," or "the 'isness' of segregation has not the 'oughtness' of the moral law," should not be allowed to obscure Christian responsibility for the purely impersonal context of a legal system which alone makes possible any life of sinful man with sinful man.

Moreover, the law sought to be applied and sought to be obeyed in Montgomery was not only some justice that ought to be but the law that is in fact the law. A very earthly justice and order was accepted, even if one Negro understandably expressed his joy over the Supreme Court's decision by exclaiming, "God Almighty has spoken from Washington, D. C."[24] Christians may not say simply that they are going to obey the will of God and not man's law, nor say that an unjust "law" is not law, since the will of God is not known to us as a system of unwritten law rivaling human law and since observance of human law is also obedience to God's will to preserve the world and in it, in spite of human sin, the possibility of any life at all of man with man. The same conclusion can be reached, in all but the most extreme circumstances, from the point of view of the state and its legal system. Here the words of Emil Brunner are to the point:

> If, as was fully the case in the mediaeval world, the "law of nature" implies that a law of the state must not be obeyed if it conflicts with the law of nature, and hence is unjust, the law of nature means an intolerable menace to the system of positive law. What enabled the error to arise, and to become more and more dangerous in its effect, was the development of the law of nature into a complete system of law which entered into competition with the positive law of the state; this has been

---

[24] Martin Luther King, *Stride Toward Freedom* (New York: Harper & Brothers, 1958), p. 160.

increasingly the case since Grotius. No state law can tolerate a competition of this kind presented by a second legal system. The laws of the state actually obtaining must possess a monopoly of binding legal force; the law of nature must claim no binding legal force for itself if the legal security of the state is to remain unshaken. That is the point at which the Reformers diverged most widely from the view of mediaeval Catholicism. They took their stand clearly on the side of positive law, granting to the law of nature the function of a criterion.[25]

It must be set down as a wholly unevangelical interpretation of man, of sin, and of the legitimate claims of social order by which anyone has come to believe that private individuals or factions or groups of individuals have a *right* to disobey human law by virtue of their appeal to a special knowledge of juster law that should, but does not, obtain.

Civil disobedience is certainly not a *legal* right, except where this is expressly allowed in law (as in provision for the status of conscientious objection to military service); and then it is no longer civil *disobedience,* but rather exceptional behavior allowed by law. Proper respect for law is not adequately stated by simply saying, "all people should obey just laws," "an unjust law is no law at all," or that respect for law means this: "The individuals engaged in sit-in demonstrations are revealing the highest respect for laws, and they respect the law so much that they want to see all laws just and in line with the moral law of the universe, and they are willing to suffer and sacri-

---

[25] *Justice and the Social Order* (New York: Harper & Brothers, 1945), p. 93.

fice in order to square local customs and local laws with the moral law of the universe."[26] The reply to these words of Martin Luther King by James Kilpatrick was certainly not correct either. While King made justice too simple and immediately available as ground for civil disobedience, Kilpatrick removed justice too far from determinations of the law when he said: "I would prefer here on earth that we tried to abide by the law of the land, by the statutes, by the court decisions, by the other acts that establish law here on earth. It will be time enough later on to get to the moral law of the universe." To Mr. King it must be said that natural justice and a "higher law" are *only* a "criterion," and to Mr. Kilpatrick it must be said that justice and the "moral law of the universe" *is*, and *is now*, the "criterion" entering in at every point in the determination of law by courts and legislators.

Certainly, it is correct to appeal to white Southerners to obey the Supreme Court's decision in the school desegregation cases as the law of the land—not only because this is just and in accord with a higher moral law, and not only because it is now legal and therefore inevitable, but also for this additional reason: that (as Kilpatrick said) "there is a pretty high degree of morality involved in simply abiding by the law." It is, therefore, a matter of some significance for morality to ask: What should be the attitude and action of a Christian

---

[26] This and following references are to the transcript of "Are Sit-In Strikes Justifiable," *The Nation's Future*, NBC-TV, November 26, 1960, in which the Rev. Martin Luther King, leader of the sit-ins, participated with James Kilpatrick, editor of the Richmond *News Leader*.

citizen following a decision of the Supreme Court determining the supreme law of the land in a fashion he regards as clearly unjust? It is not enough to assert simply that "no court has given the states the right to deny individuals their constitutional rights," and that the highest court will not do this. This is no answer to the question, when one clear legal justification of the sit-ins is that they will serve to determine what the law *is*, as this will be construed by the judiciary. The ruling of courts of appeal will precisely determine the *meaning* of "constitutional rights" in the case of service in restaurants, etc. A case will reach the Supreme Court early in 1961, arising out of a sit-in in Baton Rouge, Louisiana. Since in this instance, however, the owner did not ask that the students be arrested for trespass, no question will be raised and settled concerning a conflict between the students' rights and the property rights of the store. Instead, according to petitioners, their arrest was solely a police idea, on the charge of "disturbing the peace," under a Louisiana statute that makes it a crime to act "in such a manner as to unreasonably disturb or alarm the public." According to the *New York Times,* January 3, 1961, this case differs from other sit-in tests, and is "more favorable legally to the Negro students—because there is no charge of trespass." It will likely be resolved on the "unconstitutional vagueness" of the statute, and on the ground that when the police initiated the arrests this constituted unconstitutional "state action" to enforce segregation. A case is not yet on the docket of the Supreme Court which will require some adjudication between the rights of property owners and those of individuals in the public they are in business to serve. At the moment, decisions within the last two years by three state supreme courts and by two Circuit Courts of Appeals may be cited (as Kilpatrick did), seeming to establish some judicial precedent against the "inn keeper's law." So it is not a merely hypothetical question to ask: Should citizens and Christians participating in the sit-ins continue to do so after a possible decision that the supreme law of the land allows owners to refuse service or state and local laws to prohibit desegregated service? There would then be no *constitutional* right to refuse to leave upon request, except in states that have by legislation limited the rights of property by requiring non-discrimination in this regard.

Fortunately, for our purposes in attempting to bring into focus the moral problem of law observance, this issue will remain with us in one form or another even if the Court should rule (as is to be hoped) in the Baton Rouge case, or some other case arising out of the sit-ins, that private owners offering services for sale to the public have no such right in their property. In the case *supposed,* where the rule of law is contrary to natural justice which destines property to fellow humanity, an answer can be given which should prove applicable in other instances in which conscience is torn between the moral duty of obedience to law and the moral duty to seek a truer justice.

1. If such were the Court's decision, this would only shift to town councils and state legislatures the task of directing public property by legislation to the true ends of natural justice and fellow humanity. In large

measure, the action of individuals and groups in be-half of greater justice should likewise shift to this arena. It may in fact be true that we have come to rely too heavily on the courts to make law and to defend the rights of men. Citizens have not been alert and willing to engage constantly in the democratic process by which our society gives itself laws; and legislators have sometimes acted with scandalous irresponsibility in enacting statutes foreknown to be unconstitutional. But the shift of the struggle for greater justice from the courts to the sphere of legislation most certainly means that everyone should have effective power through voting, that all the votes must be counted and everyone must count as a voter, and no individual should be excluded from his just share in making the laws he is expected to obey. No man is good or wise enough to govern another without his consent, and no class or race of people should have their wills exclusively expressed in statutes regulating the use of public property.

2. Still there will be persons who are impelled to the conclusion that they cannot in conscience continue to obey unjust laws while taking action to change them. I assume there may be sufficient validity in such conscience, in a man's apprehensions of justice to which laws are contrary, on which he may base "conscientious objection" or "conscientious" refusal to obey. At the least, it should be clear that it would be worse for such a man to obey the law *un*conscientiously or quite contrary to the deepest integrity of his conscience—worse for him and finally worse for his community and for the state of which he is a part. I

assume, moreover, that his scruple may for him be sufficient to override, in this particular case, the degree to which law observance should still *also and at the same time* command his moral approval even with respect to an unjust law seen as still bearing in itself the rule of law as such, and certainly out of respect for law and concern for order in general. This might be called *"conscientious* conscientious objection," or *"conscientious* conscientious refusal to obey" an unjust command. This means respect for the conscience of the law as well as for a higher justice apprehended in one's own conscience. Such was the position of Socrates in relation to the laws of Athens.

Socrates drank the hemlock rather than agree in the future to conduct himself in what he regarded as an unjust manner and contrary to his basic convictions. He also knew that his was an unjust execution. Yet he acknowledged that the laws of Athens had a right to do this to him. He steadfastly refused to obey the law, and at the same time he steadfastly refused to except himself from the governance of these laws by escaping to another city and avoiding their punishment. Before his death Socrates represented the laws of Athens as speaking to him: ". . . he has made an agreement with us that he will duly obey our commands; and he neither obeys them nor convinces us that our commands are unjust; and we do not rudely impose them, but give him the alternative of convincing us;—that is what we offer and he does neither." Continuing its address to him, the conscience of the laws reminded Socrates, who was tempted to declare an unjust law to be no law at all, that the law had presided over his birth, education, and marriage and would continue to provide order for the lives of his children. "Will there be no one to remind you that in your old age you were not ashamed to violate the most sacred laws from a miserable desire for a little more life?"[27] This expresses very well the exceptional case of disobedience to law, between the main enduring alternatives of either obeying or convincing the laws that they are unjust.

Less eloquently but still in the spirit of Socrates, two living men have expressed, in connection with the sit-ins, this same understanding of the element of respect for law and effective acceptance of its legitimacy and force, which should be present in every case of *conscientious* conscientious refusal to obey laws. Hard pressed to justify sit-ins on the supposition that the law of the land had been declared by judges of our highest earthly court to be not quite identical with his own conception of the moral law of the universe, Martin Luther King remarked at one point in the nationally televised debate, "I think the individual who discovers on the basis of conscience that a law is unjust and is willing in a very peaceful sense to disobey that unjust law and *willingly and voluntarily suffers the consequences,* I think at this moment he is expressing the highest respect for law" (italics added). If suffering the consequences includes positive voluntary acceptance of the consequences that *the law* will enforce upon such a person, indeed this does mean a profound respect not only for law in general but precisely for the

27 Plato, *The Crito,* 52, 53.

particular law in question because it *is* the law and because it represents the whole legal order that stands behind it, even while one resolves never to obey it. There was, I must say, more understanding of the law as a moral ordering of human reality concentrated in these words of King than in his apparent call to a war of all sincere persons against all other sincere persons who are agreed that an unjust law is no law at all, yet who (as is to be expected) diametrically disagree in a given instance about the meaning of justice, provided only that they use the non-violent means of "civil," i.e., loving, resistance.[28]

The second recent spokesman for a point of view not wholly foreign to Socrates' words in behalf of the conscience of the laws was Thurgood Marshall: "If the Supreme Court should declare that the sit-in is unlawful and a violation of personal rights," he said, "and if there is going to be a moral problem, that's an individual's moral problem. Any individual has the right to feel that he considers it to be morally incorrect and for him to personally obey it would be to interfere with his own morals and his conscience. He has a perfect right to disobey it and he also has the right to go to jail for disobeying it. And that's my answer to the

---

[28] It is true that means and ends interpenetrate; and there is an *ethics* of means in Christian ethics. In fact, a morality of means may be more important in Christian ethics than morality focused on ends; and in democratic theory and practice, procedures may be in some sense more important than goals. Yet all this is far from saying that non-violent resistance sums up that necessary *morality of means*. The fact is that "civil disobedience" can be as devastating and unloving and irresponsible as "uncivil disobedience." Chapter three undertakes to make clear that the "just conduct" of resistance is to be defined in terms of the limited *direction* of the resistance and not alone in terms of the nature of the weapons used.

Southerner who says he has a right to oppose the Supreme Court school decision. He has the right to oppose it and he has the right to do any act he dares to do to oppose it but with the full understanding that he pays the penalty of going to jail for his opposition."[29]

Yet another component may be indicated which surely will remain relevant to any man's decision that he must conscientiously refuse to obey the existing law. This is the special poignancy involved in disobedience to specific laws that *legally define the rights of other human beings* in relation to one's own. It is one thing to throw open the windows and in plain view worship God contrary to a tyrannical edict that prohibits this. Here perhaps mainly the individual and his relation to God and to the rule of law in general are at stake. It is one thing to refuse to obey a decree which requires that one's parents be spied on and any political disaffection on their parts reported to the police, or, by not voicing one word or lifting a finger, to consent to laws that unjustly persecute people of Jewish blood. Here duties to other concrete persons are *in alliance with* one's conscientious refusal to obey unjust laws. Specific duties to others are here a part of *conscientious* conscientious disobedience.

It is quite another thing, however, to undertake direct "conscientious" action against a supposed "invasion" of the integrity of the family when the law prohibits some kinds and length of the labor a family may exact from a child. It is also quite another thing for a person out of conscientious scruple to refuse to

---

[29] "The Living Constitution—Civil Rights and the Negro," *The Open Mind*, NBC-TV, December 4, 1960.

obey compulsory vaccination laws, since this involves the rights of others to be protected from epidemics. It is another thing for a parent who is a Jehovah's Witness to assert that the law has no right to infringe his religious liberty if such conscientious refusal to obey the law means refusal to permit a blood transfusion to be given to his dying child. In general, then, *conscientious* conscientious objection should somehow acknowledge the conscience of the laws, and it should never be wholly lacking in genuine respect for the rights of others, where these are also at issue, as they are legally construed and protected in existing laws. The fact is that should the Supreme Court declare sit-in demonstrations "unlawful" it will at the same time declare them to be a violation of personal rights —the rights of owners. This would have morally to be taken into account in any refusal to obey the law.

In going beyond trying to convince the laws that they are unjust and in ever refusing to obey them, it is a twice-serious matter also to refuse the law's adjudication of rights between mine and thine. In attempting to bring into focus the moral problem of law observance, it is fortunate that, in the case we are *supposing,* the present writer and most of the readers of this volume (I trust) are agreed as to the natural justice of the matter, as Christians should view this. A Supreme Court ruling that did not limit the individual rights of owners of property for public purposes would frustrate the just ends of property right and it would be contrary to human nature as fellow humanity. But one's clear and sincere opinion that such a decision would be unjust helps to isolate and define the moral issues that remain in choosing between observance or non-observance of admittedly unjust law. We should not go so far as to say that an unjust law is no law at all. Nor should we say that a legally defined right is no right at all, simply by virtue of the fact that it is violative of our own conceptions of justice, identical as these usually seem to be with the laws of God.

I do not say that conscientious disobedience to such a ruling ought never to be undertaken; but this defines a basic factor in the conscientiousness of it and a moral restraint upon it. We should not lightly say that the conflict is between "human" rights on one side and only prejudice and "property" on the other—forgetting the respect due to be given even to the law's clumsy attempt to arrange the attainment of my rights together with the rights of other men. In a larger sense this is the meaning of the conscience of the laws as an ordering of human reality, and of respect for law as the ordering of the various claims and counterclaims men put forward as the meaning of justice in regard to them. Legal definition of rights is needed to adjust rival claims, *especially* where one party or another is quite *certain* about the justice of the matter. The subjective aspect of the function of law in ordering human relationships is the respect a person should give to law especially when his own claims to justice are limited or his own cause not fully endorsed by legal enactment or judicial decision. This means in some fashion a positive response to the conscience of the laws. This may require a mantle of charity thrown around the rights of others, and perhaps a mantle of doubt about a person's own competence, alone or uncorrected by other contending judgements, to know what is just in case of a conflict between his own conscience and the consciences of other men. Of course, in one sense a man cannot doubt the conviction of his own conscience and at the same time act upon these same convictions. But in a profounder sense, precisely this can and should be done—by using natural justice and the dictates of conscience as a "criterion," by not exalting these standards into an accessible code of law in direct and triumphant competition with existing law to the displacement of the latter as in no sense obligatory, and by finding some way of acknowledging the conscience of the laws especially as that conscience may be contained in its adjustment of the rights men (and *I* especially) claim with and against man. Thus, conscientious resistance, properly understood, appeals to natural justice or to a higher law as a "criterion" only and not yet as *law,* no less than natural justice should serve as goal and standard and criterion in one's attempt to convince the laws, in the determination of what law should be and in the struggle for greater justice enacted into law through the legislative process. Thus a Christian responds obediently both to law and to the claims of natural justice as this may be illuminated by Christ to his conscience. His appeal is to justice as a criterion in seeking to transform the laws, or in only forming his own attitude and action with regard to laws he must regard as so unjust he cannot obey them and still remain a man. In the midst of this appeal to transcendent justice, he at the same time submits his views to judgment in dialogue with the views of others as people together go about giving themselves law. When he decides he must stand out and resist or not obey law, he still submits his own attitude and action to judgment by the laws which have been enacted by this same process of convincing one another and the laws. He does this because he knows that his own conscience provides the criterion and is not itself law, and because he does not exempt himself or his most clear convictions from the need of possible correction. Such is the Christian understanding of the rule of law, justice as criterion, and of the need for order.

This meaning was implicit in the long centuries of the Christian tradition in interpreting the law so as to assign to the topmost official or prince (never irresponsible power, but) the responsibility to make use of the "law of nature" or the norm of natural justice as a "criterion." The highest government official *himself* decided the justice of the cause before him for adjudication and he governed the people by laws that had a monopoly of binding legal force, submissive only to the function of the "natural law" as "a criterion" directing him in the fashioning of law. It is true, and quite important for the political life of the West, that the Reformation initiated that development in politics by which the "magisterial capacity" (formerly the prince's only) to apply the "criterion" of natural law came to rest upon the head and in the actions of the ordinary citizen. Thereafter the people generally participated in the decision-making process by which laws are enacted and shaped to be more in accord with the norm of natural justice. The "citizen" is a former "magistrate." But this gave him the capacity and right to share in the making of law, not any right to break law on his own private authority. It is true also that Protestantism, e.g., Calvinism, spoke of the *right* of resistance against tyranny or grave injustice; but this was to be exercised only in extreme circumstances and with large acceptance of the claims of order (theologically understood) in human affairs. An individual had a right to resist only as a "lesser magistrate" or in an assumed "magisterial capacity"; and this meant that even revolution was viewed as an extreme case of his participation in the magisterial power and duty to consult natural justice as a criterion in making laws and preserving order, which ordinarily should be done while continuing to obey even the unjust laws he is attempting to reshape through established legal procedures for doing so.

Where states have become wholly totalitarian, where the means for changing laws have become clogged and men wholly frustrated in their search for legal justice, there the so-called "natural law" and the will of our God who purposes fellow humanity do mean for the Christian that there is a *moral* right of disobedience to law, a right of resistance (and prudence alone, and not any intrinsic difference between violent and nonviolent means, determines that this may not take the form of a right of revolution). But no legal system (tyrannical or more or less just) can tolerate the idea that there is a system of non-legal law or rules of natural justice, in competition with the positive law, and directly accessible to individuals or groups or individuals within the state, which should prevail over and have more binding force than the law of the land. This is the reason no legal system contains the *legal* right to disobey, to resist, or to overturn the law by direct action or by revolution.[30] Instead, in democratic societies, the moral right to resist and not co-operate with injustice takes form in the various legal ways in which citizens may engage in changing the law. In this sense, democracy means justifiable and limited resistance (and thus it refines and establishes procedures for making a justifiable revolution, which is in principle to apply in domestic politics the same line of reasoning that drove Christians in the early centuries of this era to justify and limit warfare for the resistance and correction of evil). The operation in any legal system of procedures for transforming the law and thus to resist and not ultimately accept or co-operate with evil or injustice emphasizes all the more the duty every citizen has to observe and obey the law.

This is also why, we said earlier, it is precisely for the sake of preserving the social order that there needs to be a rapid achievement of greater justice in the common life, and especially in race relations a greater agreement of wills that constitute us one nation.

---

30 The enactment of a status for "conscientious objection" to military service, or the granting of citizenship to avowed pacifists, is no exception to this. However much a part of American law such provisions may now be, they are always by grace of an act of Congress, which, if it has the power to do this, has also the legal power not to do so. Apart from this, a Christian who had to decide in conscience not to obey military conscription should also understand (if his mind is clear in what he is doing and his action a fully responsible one) that the cause of the order of his whole national community will be staked (even if in very unenlightened fashion) when the full force of the law returns upon his civil disobedience. The exercise of his *moral* right of disobedience, not having been granted legal status (which then would mean that it is not disobedience), has as its obverse side the state's right to inflict penalty for disobedience.

A nation in which conscientious people in great numbers are driven to the violation of unjust laws they see no way of changing, e.g., the fugitive slave laws, is already a nation on the way to civil strife. There needs always to be among us a lively concern to keep open and to perfect the ways in which individuals and groups of people may share in refashioning the law by which they are governed. Rule 22 of the U. S. Senate, and the way control is exercised by the Rules Committee of the House of Representatives in directing the traffic of bills to that legislative body, may be cited as blocks in the way of the protection of human rights and establishment of greater justice in race relations in this country. In reforming these legislative procedures, however, the Christian is one who knows that even such rules and procedures doubtless restrain and remedy some forms of human sinfulness which without them would be without let or hindrance. He will urge the revision of them, however radically, only with this in mind, and because it is now clear that the procedure in question partakes more of an imperialism of power in the legislative process frustrating justice than there is imperialism in the power it represses from also frustrating justice, say, by an unqualified and unlimited and immediate enactment of the majority's will upon every subject that comes before the Senate, or by the autocratic authority of the Speaker of the House which the Rules Committee was originally designed to correct. Thus do the requirements of order and of justice always go together in the Christian view of man's life with man.

Many of these considerations were summed up in

an admirable statement by some of the Faculty of the Divinity School of Vanderbilt University, April 8, 1960, setting forth their position in the Lawson case. Before we come, in the next chapter, to the specific issue of the Christian use of economic pressures in attempting to influence race relations, a few paragraphs from this statement may be quoted in concluding our discussion of the Christian understanding of the principles of political action:

A vital principle to us is that progress and liberty for all races and groups is best served by an orderly, dependable governmental process. Accordingly, we commend to our students and to others with whom we have influence an attitude of respect for law and patience in situations where justice seems to take its time. We also believe that isolated laws are occasionally enforced for unconstitutional and immoral purposes; and we would support the right of individuals to test such laws by deliberate violation. We would not interfere, however, to prevent such individuals from being apprehended and punished by the civil authorities, since those who violate laws, even for the sake of conscience, must be prepared to take the consequences meted by the judicial arm of government. At the same time, we would note that the responsibility of dealing with such violators of law belongs to civil authorities; we would assume that the University in which such students are enrolled would neither protect them, nor act against them.

In a situation where civil authorities state that a student's actions endanger the public peace, we would expect the University to co-operate with the authorities. However, pending judicial proceedings to determine the student's innocence or guilt we would hope that the University might refrain from taking action which would definitely terminate the status of the accused as a student. Not even a verdict of guilty, we suggest, should invariably entail, in every case, expulsion from the University. In any event, we would hope that the University can agree that not every illegal action is necessarily an immoral one, and thus that the right of conscience can be protected by the University at least up to the point where civil authorities themselves feel compelled to take action.[31]

We repeat that our purpose is to commend lawful and orderly methods of securing social justice.

This concludes the basic analysis of this chapter. Before closing, however, *where* and *why* and to what extent this analysis of the question of legality may fail to apply to the sit-in should be made very clear. The duty to observe the law, we have said, has full force only where people of any race in our society effectively have the vote, and can participate politically at the state and local levels in the changing of undesirable local ordinances or discriminatory

---

[31] The first part of this sentence may be queried. Certainly not every illegal action is therefore never to be done. But in what has gone before it has been made clear that legality and illegality are also a moral question for Christian ethics; and how this is so has been explained. Certainly, there can be no direct and simple appeal to a moral code, accessible to conscience, displacing the actual law from governance of the political order.

We do not enter upon a discussion of a subordinate question that also faced the faculty and administration of Vanderbilt, and which is referred to in the latter part of the sentence above. This is the question whether a "lesser corporation" such as university has any responsibility in doing the work of the state and of the law, or for anticipating it by expulsion. Generally and perhaps always the answer should be negative. But to show that this is a genuine problem, and not a fabricated one, we might suppose a man, with status as a student in the university, who is engaged in direct action using economic pressure to prevent Negroes from registering to vote, and legal action has been begun to prevent this. The present writer would also in this instance want to endorse the judgment of the Vanderbilt faculty that a university is not an arm of the law.

state statutes. Every man must have political initiative as a "minor magistrate." His magisterial capacity as a citizen should make it possible for him to participate democratically in making the laws, applying in his own right the "criterion" of natural justice to help determine the legal requirements. Anyone who would cast out the members of any race from exercising the franchise, from participating in democratic discussion leading to consent to laws, and from running for public office or from leadership in the community, cannot then with clean hands and a clean heart insist that they should still be law-abiding people, for the theological, ethical, and political reasons given in this chapter. The white people of this country can regard it as fortunate that the participants in the sit-in movement, as *direct action* which *may* be against the laws, so largely share in the tradition of "law and order," and that they are imbued with the spirit of charity in the tactical form of non-violent resistance. This gives us time rapidly to include them not in passive consent only but in active consent to the laws that govern us all, by positive participation in the rights of citizens to rule, as formerly only magistrates did, in a democratic society, and to help determine the justice of any law that *is* a law. As we go forward toward these goals, it may be well for us to have in mind a word of warning and a word of hope. The warning is contained in Thomas Jefferson's statement: "I tremble for my country when I think of the Negro and remember that God is just." This warning has hope on its other side; and this was expressed by Pearl Buck: "We have another asset, and it is in the colored people of the United States. We Americans are singularly fortunate, if we only knew it, in having ten per cent of our people colored. It gives Americans a chance to get ready for the future."[32]

---

[32] *New York Times Magazine*, May 31, 1942.

3

The Christian Use of Economic Pressure
to Transform Race Relations

So far the meaning of justice and of human rights
has been viewed as resting upon the foundation of the
created order. This has been explained to mean the
duality of one man directly with and for another
man. This is the most basic form of man's fellow
humanity and it fixes covenant existence as the destiny
of human life. It is now necessary, upon the basis of
this primary duality of man's relation with his single
neighbor, to take into account the fact that in actuality a man always stands together with many others
in various groups organized for a common purpose
and simultaneously in responsible multilateral relation to many neighbors. Each of these fellow men has
equal claim upon him (when these are regarded one
by one) to be with them through justice and for them
in Christian love. This is the full context in which
the question of the use of economic pressure in the
transformation of race relations arises for the Christian.

Fellow humanity, or the requirements of justice
upon man with other men, as well as the responsibili-
ties of men in the order of charity are in and of themselves non-preferential in outlook. In either case, so

far as the agent alone is concerned, he should not discriminate among fellow men but would seek to live with all God's human creatures and for any man to the benefit of all for whom Christ died. Nevertheless, our first statement concerning the external possibility and internal actuality of existence in covenant with all the companions God gives us in any actual life situation must be that fellow humanity can and may and should find sufficient reason in particular actions for differentiating among men and for preferring to serve one cause rather than another. Our second statement must be that such differentiation in particular moments among our fellow men, and preference for one cause rather than another in action about to be put forth in support of greater justice in the established relationships among men, should always be with and for fellow humanity in such a way as to include also the fellow humanity of all the persons—even the "enemy"—who are now resisted or placed under pressures of one sort or another.

The Principle of "Justifiable" Resistance

Always this has been the premise of Christian social ethics; and in this regard it is important to understand that the jusification of resistance and the use of pressure (and, even more basic, the preference for one man over another, however ungodly) have been the problem for Christian conscience. The problem has *not* been the particular kind of resistance or pressure about to be used. This can be illustrated by the definite fashioning of principles of justice by divine charity in the concept of the *justum bellum,* or the specifications for "justifiable" warfare, in the early centuries of the church, and in the whole tradition of civilized warfare to which this gave rise and effect in the West until our present post-Christian and correspondingly barbaric times. Love and mercy, Christians believe, are the fulfilling of the law, of natural justice, and of the meaning expressed in the commandment, "Thou shalt not kill." The Christians who formulated the just war theory were driven to make in this regard one, single, clearly defined and limited *exception*. That was what it was, an exception —nothing more. Those persons "formally" directing or participating in the military forces, or "materially" yet closely co-operating in the force that should be repelled and can be repelled only by violent means— these persons are, this theory states, legitimate objects of *direct* violent repression.

What was the reason for this conclusion? What was the motivation for and shaping influence upon this exception? And when these questions are answered, must we not say that the justification of limited warfare was not actually an exception but instead an expression of the Christian understanding of fellow humanity? For in that ancient theory of just war, Christian conscience took the form of allowing any killing at all of men for whom Christ died only because military personnel were judged to stand, factually or objectively, at the point where there converged many multilateral relations of a Christian to his neighbors, at the point of the intersection of many primary dualities of his life with and for fellow man. While, of course, this included undiminished fellow humanity with the enemy soldier, the claims of many others had also to be acknowledged and realistically served in the only way possible. In this world and not some other, covenant must be enacted. Out of neighbor-regarding love for all one's fellow men, preferential decision among one's neighbors may and can and should be made. For love's sake (the very principle of the prohibition of killing) Christian thought and action were driven to posit this single exception (an exception only when externally viewed): that forces should be repelled and the bearers and close co-operators in military force should be directly repressed, by violent means if necessary, lest many more of God's little ones should be irresponsibly forsaken and lest they suffer more harm than need be. This, then, was not really an "exception" but a determinate expression of justice and mercy. It was, and is, a *regrettably* necessary but still a *necessary* expression of fellow humanity.

Non-Violent Resistance: Sit-Ins and Boycotts

The same has to be said in the case of a Christian's analysis of the ethical issues in his use of economic pressures to transform race relations. Here non-resisting love can and may and must find a way to prefer at the moment to enhance the status of some rather than others of our fellow men in the fabric of the common life and a way of resisting the will and ways of these others. Such is the premise and the analysis, indeed, of action within a democracy and within its legal procedures for changing the law for the purpose of resisting and defeating the will and way of anyone or the members of any faction with whom also we share a fellow humanity. No teacher in Galilee taught us to resist them by ballots but not by bullets. The question to be resolved is how non-resisting love can take form as its apparent opposite, namely, resistance by ballots, non-violent resistance by the pressures exerted by sit-ins or economic boycotts, or in international relations resistance by armed violence. Only in an abstract world can a significant distinction be made between resisting *discrimination* while not resisting or coercing the *people* who discriminate.[1] One cannot let go the ballot at the evil of discrimination while withholding an intention to defeat those who discriminate. He cannot let go the coercive force of sit-ins or boycotts against customs or legally-protected, impersonal rights of property, while withholding the intention to oppose, with resistance and non-violent force, the evil-doers who are property owners and *men* whose convictions and practices alike may be unjust. He can do these things no more than a bombardier can let go his explosives against the im-

---

[1] Cf. my *Basic Christian Ethics* (New York: Charles Scribner's Sons, 1950), pp. 168-9: "Although his words were, 'Do not resist *one* who is evil,' Jesus did not even draw out very explicitly the distinction between resisting *evil* and not resisting the evil-*doer*, between condemning 'the system' and denouncing people who support it, which Christians often insist was his meaning. The evil and the one who does it are in any actual situation bound so closely together that a person who, in one-one relationship to an enemy-neighbor, wishes not to resist the evil-doer can find no way of resisting evil; and a person in multilateral relationships with more than one neighbor who wishes for their sakes to resist evil will be unable to avoid resisting the evil-doer as well. With prophetic indignation, therefore, Jesus denounced those who were evil as well as impersonal forms of evil itself. This he did from neighbor-centered preferential love, although as far as his life alone was concerned he showed no preference for his own personal welfare and did not resist evil-doers when evil fell upon him."

personal power of a nation ranged, he believes, against the cause of justice, while attempting inwardly the act of withholding the intention to kill people. The question to be resolved is, therefore, how non-resisting love can take up resistance (or rather how it can remain love concretely devoted to life with and for fellow man *without* taking up resistance). In comparison with this fundamental issue, questions about the nature and type of resistance to be used are always secondary and tactical (although not, for this reason, without ethical significance).

The resistance of the evil ones by ballots is a justifiable inference drawn in Christian conscience and only in face of the fact that the multiple claims of men converge upon us and call for responsible decision among them while we strive to achieve an order of life that as far as possible includes all. As was suggested above, democracy itself in a very real sense is nothing more than *justum bellum,* both in its origin in Western history and in the principles of Christian ethics requiring participation in it as a form of regularized struggle between man and man in the midst of which alone we have in this fallen world any life with man preserved unto a higher and more open fellowship.

Such, then, would be a sound Christian understanding of the use of various forms of economic pressure, e.g., strikes, boycotts, etc., in order to bend and reshape local custom and practices in race relations. These types of direct social action should conform to the ancient principles and limitations justifying a Christian in taking up any use of force. These principles can be stated in terms of (1) the justifiability of using economic pressure, and (2) the limitation upon the economic pressures employed, or, respectively, what a love-transformed and transforming justice permits to be done and what this still requires to be not done in any area of conflict between man and man.

1. In the economic and social order there are persons who are the principle bearers or agents in unjust practices or who are close material co-operators in that injustice. These may have to be directly coerced in the struggle for justice, since pressures brought to bear upon them may be the only way to attack the impacted, customary injustice that should be resisted and changed for the sake of fellow humanity. The economic boycott of their segregated businesses; picket lines of protests in front of their stores to arouse the community, to induce people not to trade with them, and to compel them to change their policies: these things are quite in order. This need not mean that the proprietor is, in a moral and personal sense, more "guilty" of the injustice in question than other people in the community. He may only fear a greater loss of trade if he changes his practice. Still he stands objectively at the point where some form of pressure needs to be exerted if the unjust force and pressures of social habit that should be corrected are to be overcome and changed. No more did the theory of just war imply that military personnel were more "guilty" in a personal sense than others. Still they were combatants whose deeds had to be repressed.

2. The economic pressure employed should be

limited *in its target*. This limitation is implicitly contained in the justification of any use of economic pressures to effect social change. The same fellow humanity which permits the use of direct pressure upon the agents in and through whom injustice is objectively done by segregation in hotels and restaurants, also requires that these forms of force be not intentionally directed nor objectively done directly to the economic injury of people not directly responsible for, or closely co-operating in, the evil sought to be changed. These are "non-combatants" in the struggle for justice; and they are not legitimate targets of *direct* repression or economic injury—however much it may be admitted that some of these may be as subjectively guilty as anybody else in approving of segregation, and no matter how much many of them may have *indirectly* and *secondarily* to suffer economically from a successful boycott rightly directed against those in the forefront of the unjust practices that should be removed. Moreover, in addition to limiting the pressure in its direct objective to the principle bearers and close co-operators in the injustice sought to be corrected, responsible Christian action would seek to limit as far as possible the extent to which the indirect effects of the direct action taken fall upon anyone else who is not the primary bearer of the injustice that should be corrected.

There is contained here a moral distinction between primary and secondary boycotts, which need not be spelled out in specific detail. An illustration, however, may be given. Boycotts against stores practicing segregation at their lunch counters, and against the white citizens of Tuskegee, Alabama, who have directly supported political gerrymandering to deny Negroes the right to vote in municipal elections, are certainly to be justified. But, *on the supposition* that the proprietor and the employees of a local Woolworth store in New York City have not a share in formulating the policies of the chain as a whole, nor in determining the policies of a Woolworth store located in North Carolina, a Christian use of economic pressure may and should be mounted against the proprietor in North Carolina and not against the proprietor in New York City, who is twice removed from the practices in need of correction. While admitting that, even so, economic injury will be suffered by persons not directly responsible for maintaining this policy, still economic injury may not be deliberately and directly done to other persons as a *means* of getting at the persons who are responsible for the policy sought to be corrected. Indiscriminating boycotts are the moral equivalent of obliterating people in warfare in order to get at their government, or to a direct attack upon a man's wife and children in order to restrain his own murderous intent—although it has to be admitted that there may be situations in which their lives may have to be placed in indirect but real and foreknown jeopardy in order to restrain him.

Assemblage for public protest and to manifest sympathy for and support of the sit-ins in the South should take the form, not of direct economic action against persons not directly involved in segregation, but in public parks, meeting halls, etc. Such was the action taken by the students and faculty of the Yale Divinity

School in marching *en masse* down to the "village green" in New Haven for a rally, and addressing themselves to the immediate improvement of race relations in that city. The achievement of the desegregation of certain lunch counters not only by wise action by local community leaders but by voluntary action following consultation between Attorney General Rogers and the heads of certain national chain stores should, of course, be applauded. But for it to be just to attain this same result by means of the force of a boycott throughout the nation would require the verification of facts contrary to those assumed in the foregoing case. The suppositions in the previous illustration might be sufficiently altered by establishing a connection between general company practice and local practice in the South, and by establishing such direct connection between the practice and the economic well-being of stores located in New York and general company policy. Then the boycott would not be secondary, but a primary one. It would be directed against the actual location of the unjust policy which, for love's sake and for the sake of justice, must be removed, and, indivisible from this, to the economic injury of the people directly and objectively a part of this policy. Perhaps this would be sufficient to justify an economic boycott of an entire national chain in order, by threatening potential injury to its entire economy, to effect an alteration of the policy of its local stores in the matter of segregation. Such a general boycott might still be a blunt or indiscriminating instrument, and therefore of questionable justification. Action located where the evil is concentrated will prove most decisive and is most clearly legitimate. Moreover, prudence alone would indicate that, unless the local customs are already ready to fall when pushed, the results of direct economic action everywhere upon national chain stores will likely be simply to give undue advantage to local and state stores which conform to these customs, leading to greater decentralization and local autonomy within the company, or even (as the final self-defeat of an unjust application of economic pressure to correct injustice) to its going out of business in certain sections of the country (as, for that matter, the Quakers, who once had many meetings in the pre-Civil War South, largely went out of business in that part of the country over the slavery issue, never to recover a large number of southern adherents).

In any case, anyone who fails to make significant distinction between primary and secondary applications of economic pressure would in principle already have justified that use of economic boycott as a means which broke out a few years ago or was skillfully organized by White Citizens' Councils in the entire state of Mississippi against every local Philco dealer in that state, in protest against a Philco-sponsored program over a national TV network on which was presented a drama showing, it seemed, a "high yellow gal" smooching with a white man. It is true, of course, that the end or objective of this action was different. But since this is a world in which people disagree about ends and goals and concerning justice and injustice, and since, in a situation where direct action and economic pressure are called for, the justice of the matter has either not been clearly defined by law or the law is not effectively present, there has to be a *morality of means* applied in every case in which people take it upon themselves to use economic pressures or other forms of force.

The need that we not give unqualified approval to any but a limited use of economic pressure directed against the actual doers of injustice is clear also in light of the fact that White Citizens' Councils seem resolved to maintain segregation mainly by the use of these same means and not ordinarily by physical violence. An unlimited use of economic pressures for diametrically opposite causes could devastate the preconditions of any fellow humanity as surely as this would be destroyed by the use of more obviously brutal means. The end or aim of the action, of course, is also important, especially where it is not alone a matter of changing community customs but of the use of deadly economic power to intimidate a person from stepping forward to claim his legal rights, e.g., against Negroes who register to vote in Fayette County, Tennessee, at the present moment. Here the recourse is in steps to give economic sustenance to those being despoiled, and to legal remedies. This, however, is sufficient to show that more or less non-violent resistance and economic conflict (if both sides are strong enough) can be war of all against all no less than if other means are used. It is also sufficient to show the Christian and any other champion of justice that he needs to make sure not only that his cause is just but also that his *conduct* is just, i.e., that, if economic pressure has to be resorted to, this be applied directly against those persons directly in the way of some salutary change in business or institutional practices, while, if injury fall upon others, it fall upon them indirectly and secondarily (however inevitably) and not by deliberate intent and direct action against them.

It is clear that non-violent resistance is a mode of action in need of justification and limitation in Christian morality, like any other form of resistance. The *language* used itself often makes very clear that this is only another form of struggle for victory (perhaps to be chosen above all others). One of the sit-in leaders has said: "Nobody from the top of Heaven to the bottom of Hell can stop the march to freedom. Everybody in the world today might as well make up their minds to march with freedom or freedom is going to march over them." The present writer certainly agrees with that statement, and would also affirm this—in the order of justice. However, it is also a Christian insight to know that unless charity interpenetrates justice it is not likely to be freedom that marches forward. And when charity interpenetrates man's struggle for justice and freedom it does not simply surround this with a sentimental good will. It also definitely fashions conduct in the way explained above, and this means far more than in the choice of non-violent means. R. B. Gregg has written that "non-violence and good will of the victim act like the lack of physical opposition by the user of physical jiu-jitsu, to cause the attacker to lose his moral balance. He suddenly and unexpectedly loses the moral support which the usual violent resistance of most victims would render him"; and again,

that "the object of non-violent resistance is partly anal-
ogous to this object of war—namely, to demoralize the
opponent, to break his will, to destroy his confidence,
enthusiasm, and hope. In another respect it is dis-
similar, for non-violent resistance demoralizes the opponent only to re-establish in him a new morale that
is firmer because it is based on sounder values."[2]

A trial of strength, however, is made quite inevitable
by virtue of the fact that anyone engaging in non-
violent resistance will be convinced that his action is
based on sounder values than those of his opponent;
and in warfare with any means, men commonly disagree over the justice of the cause. This makes necessary a morality of means, and principles governing the
conduct of resistance whenever this is thought to be
justified. The question, then, is whether sufficient discrimination in the use of even non-violent means of
coercion is to be found in the fact that such conduct
demoralizes and overcomes the opponent while re-
moralizing and re-establishing him. Here it is relevant
to remember that men commonly regard some causes
as more important than their lives; and to them it will
seem insignificant that it is proposed to defeat such
causes non-violently. A technique by which it is proposed to enter with compulsion into the very heart of
a man and determine his values may often in fact
seem the more unlimited aggression.

Among Christian groups, the Mennonites have commonly been aware more than others of the fact that
the nature of divine charity raises decisively the ques-

---

[2] *The Power of Non-Violence* (New York: Fellowship Publica-
tions, 1944), pp. 43, 89.

tion of the Christian use of all forms of pressure. Since the will and word of God are for them concentrated in Christlike love, it seems clear to them that non-violent resistance is quite another thing. "The primary objective of non-violence," writes the outstanding Mennonite ethicist, "is not peace, or obedience to the divine will, but rather certain desired social changes, for personal, or class, or national advantage."[3] Without agreeing with every phrase in this statement, we must certainly assert the great difference between Christian love and any form of resistance, and then go on beyond the Mennonite position and affirm that Christian love-in-action must first justify and then determine the moral principles limiting resistance. These principles we have now set forth. *Economy* in the use of power needs not only to be asserted, but clearly specified; and when this is done it will be found that the principles governing Christian resistance cut across the distinction between violent and non-violent means, and apply to both alike, justifying either on occasion and always limiting either action. Economy in the use of power means more than inflicting a *barely intolerable* pressure upon an opponent and upon the injustice opposed. That would amount to calculating the means and justifying them wholly in terms of their effectiveness in reaching desired goals. There must also be additional and more fundamental discrimination in the use of means of resistance, violent or non-violent. The justification in Christian conscience of the use of any mode of resistance also lays down its limitation—in

---

[3] Guy F. Hershberger, *War, Peace and Nonresistance* (Scottdale, Penn.: Herald Press, 1944), p. 225.

the distinction between the persons against whom pressure is primarily directed, those upon whom it may be permitted also to fall, and those who may never be directly repressed for the sake even of achieving some great good. In these terms, the "economic withdrawal" of the Negroes of Nashville, Tennessee, from trading in the center city, for example, was clearly justified, since these distinctions do not require that only people subjectively guilty be singled out.

We may now take up for consideration a hard case which seems to require either no action employing economic pressure or else action that would seem to violate the principles set forth above. There may be instances in which, if economic pressure is to be undertaken at all, this would have to be applied without discrimination against a whole people. An excellent article was published recently in the journal of the Church Peace Union by a South African journalist on the inhuman economic conditions of the blacks in South Africa, amounting to virtual slavery, and the economic *complicity* of both the government and the people of the United States in these conditions.[4] ". . . Billions of American dollars, not only from capital investors but also from the pockets of U. S. taxpayers," this author states, "are being poured into South Africa to support a system dedicated to the oppression, the persecution, and the almost diabolical exploitation of 12 million people the color of whose skins happens not to be white." Both the conditions

---

[4] Sean Boud, "The Economics of Apartheid: The Facts are a Challenge to the Conscience of America," *Worldview,* Vol 3, No. 7-8 (July-August, 1960), pp. 3 7.

and the complicity are documented in considerable detail. This leads to the conclusion that "the fact is inescapable that America does have a say in whether or not *apartheid* shall continue." Our leadership in a wide economic boycott of South Africa would be not only in accord, it seems, with the moral conscience of America, not to be denied because we also as a people have widespread injustice in the relations of the races in our own country, but also in accord with our law, U.S. Code Title 19, Section 1307, which forbids the importation of goods made by forced or convict labor. Not only should this provision be enforced but other economic and political actions might be taken which, this author believes, "must surely be supported by every American who values the freedom that has been won for him and whose conscience is not so dominated by the lines in his account books that he can willingly and knowingly contribute to the enslavement of another nation."

Unfortunately, the issue of the justifiability of a widespread boycott in this instance is not entirely settled—though this is relevant—by the fact that "Africans in the Union have long discussed the question of what they would *like* the policy of other states to be in regard to South Africa. They have asked for as wide as possible a boycott of South African goods." Nor is it settled by the fact that Mr. Absalom Vilakasi, a leading African spokesman, can be quoted to this effect: "We know that a boycott will hurt us too, but we can bear it with a wry smile as we will know that, for once, the Nationalist Government are suffering, too." What people would like does not alone settle ethical issues. Can we say that counter-people economic warfare would be justified because this would at the same time be counter-forces warfare and would put pressure on the government, the white community, and the political leaders who make policy?

Politics, of course, and especially international political action, must be the science of the possible. It also is an area of deferred repentance—but not forever. If there has been no propitious moment yet in recent history for the United States to take action, or to cease daily to take the actions described in this article, that moment may soon come when, in concert with the other nations of the world, and especially in concert with the newer nations of Africa, our country can no longer defer making effective repentance for its complicity in injustice. Then we will face questions as to the use of strong and definite economic pressures with the purpose of radically assisting in the transformation of the whole structure of race relations in a country abroad. The moral issues here do not primarily revolve around whether or not one nation should interfere in the domestic affairs of another. Rank injustice is never exclusively a domestic matter; and the fact is that, by constant action originating in the United States, we are inexorably involved in supporting economically the domestic policies of the present South African government.

The chief ethical issue is whether a widespread international boycott is a limited, discriminating instrument to use, and whether it is justifiable if it is not. This is an extremely complex situation (now, also, to the fore in the relations of the United States and other American nations to Cuba[5] and the Dominican Republic), and a minimum of ethical analysis may be all that can be brought to bear upon the subject. Two comments may be in order.

1. The first is that no Christian should be so infatuated by the difference between non-violent and violent resistance as to be beguiled into forgetting that this is not the same as the difference between total war by any means and a limited application of power primarily against those who objectively stand at the point where injustice reigns or closely cooperate in its maintenance. A total use of economic blockade as a blunt instrument against a whole people is only prudentially different from total war with metropolis-busters—though in the same breath it should be said that expediency often draws distinctions that are of importance for morality. Economic pressures should therefore always be used with extreme care. We must not engage in the use of wholesale economic pressure directly intended and directly done against an entire people in order incidentally

---

[5] Our unilateral action placing a general embargo on the sale of all goods (except food and medical supplies) to Castro's Cuba may well have been an act of too non-discriminating counter-people economic warfare; and the injustice of this, as well as the fact that there is an order of justice amid the power relations of nations, may manifest itself in that the chief effects of this action are likely to be a certain solidification of the Cuban people behind the government sought to be restrained and a greater dependence of the Cuban economy and Cuba politically on the Communist countries (if these countries are able and willing to avail themselves of the opportunity thus provided) sought to be prevented by this action. Effective, discriminating exertions of power are also just; and just conduct is discriminating. The violent overthrow or defeat of a government may be an unjust action not because violence is used, but if and because this has associated with it both violent and "non-violent" forms of injuring people indiscriminately in order to bring their government to terms.

and indirectly to strike at the policies of their government. Instead, whatever foreseeable injury befalls the people in general should be the indirect even if certain effect of action directly intended and directly done against the central government itself and against its primary bases in the economy, while limiting as far as possible, rather than attempting to widen, the incidental consequences of economic blockade to include people who can in no sense be termed co-operators in the injustice that should be changed. A basic South African industry might be selected by injuring which would bring penalty and pressure to bear primarily upon the makers of *apartheid* policy, while its foreknown and quite dire but still secondary effects would fall on the people in general only indirectly. The pressure can be selectively begun and increased. At the same time it should be made clear, in concert with other nations, that we stand ready to help by food and other supplies to care for the immediate needs of people caught in the economic line of fire; and that the conditions would be fulfilled for a withdrawal of these pressures by a moderate-enough but definite change of governmental policy and by the adoption of deliberate steps in the direction of greater justice. No nation or concert of states should assume, simply because given the interrelatedness of the world's economy we have the means to bring enormous pressure to bear, that this gives us either the right or the power to guarantee justice with order in South Africa.

2. Secondly, a sound analysis should indicate that in all such instances we have come close to the point

where injustice and tyranny have grown so great that almost any social order is better than the existing order; but that, while this may in fact be the case, this is by no means the same thing as saying that disorder is better than the present unjust order. The primacy of order to justice, and, as we have indicated, of tolerable justice to any order, can never be forgotten by the Christian who knows the basic conditions for the external possibility of any fellow humanity's being assured under God's governance of this sinful world. Man's life with man may be preserved in pretty shoddy clothing, but not with no garments at all to cover the nakedness of man against man.

So far we have spoken of the ethical issues that arise in the participation of *anyone* in the struggle for the attainment of a more just social order: by using democratic procedures to change law; by initiating litigation in the courts to invoke the law or to determine more clearly the meaning of human rights in a given concrete situation; by protest assemblage to influence public opinion; and by bringing economic pressures to bear in an effort to batter down practices of injustice that are customary. A final word, perhaps, should be said concerning the case in which the person who does these things is not just *anyone* but a victim who suffers such injustice. How shall his action be understood from a Christian point of view? Should not his external action as well as his inward heart be characterized by suffering, reconciling love? Granting that *others,* on his behalf, ought to be able to discriminate between the primary doers and the recipients of injustice, granting that others should prefer objectively the cause of some against the will and way of others of his fellow men and should enter the struggle for justice out of fellow humanity and love for all for whom Christ died, how can a victim of injustice, who also is a Christian, for his own sake enter the world of claims and counter-claims and fail to make manifest his life with and for man in the primary form of renouncing claims for himself? In answer to this question, we may say, in the words of Emil Brunner, "If, as a good Christian," anyone "is willing to endure the injustice of his position—so far as he is concerned—for the sake of others he ought not to do so."[6]

Perhaps probing more deeply and explaining this "for the sake of others" to be not only the acceptance of external relations of responsibility in the cause of justice, we may say that no one who bears the human countenance has the right to hide this from us. He has no right to stand hat in hand and not show forth the human countenance to the full measure that it is upon him. He has no right to deprive any one or all of his fellow men of the challenge to covenant which his creation constitutes. Any failure on his part to enact his fellow manhood is not only his loss; it is a deprivation of the cause between man and man that has not been committed entirely to him alone. His inalienable right of fellow humanity is at the same time his inalienable duty to fellow man. He can never renounce this without going frontally against covenant imprinted upon him in creation and

---

[6] *The Divine Imperative* (New York: The Macmillan Co., 1937), p. 431.

depriving another of the right not to be without him. It is not permitted him to allow another to be without him. This was God's meaning when He created him and let him loose on this planet. Our God who from eternity resolved not to be God without this man thereby resolved that no other of His creatures should be men without him. He no more has the right to hide his human countenance from us than we have to deprive him of it. Our God who lets the light of this countenance fall upon us gives us this man to face us and to complete our fellow humanity both by the benefit and by the challenge of the fact that he is, and lifts up his face.

This is the great thing that has happened in the sit-ins led by Negro students. They have fulfilled the promise of covenant; they have made their humanity more fully visible; they have resolved to be there with their fellow men even if in some measure against them; they have had the courage to establish better external conditions for the possibility of man's life with man. Any failure to do this would have been a failure in them or on their side of that fellow humanity which belongs to all God's human creatures, and belongs exclusively to neither person in covenant to elect to give or withhold. The human countenance needs not to be hidden but shown forth, whether the question at issue is a definition of legal rights, or of natural justice, or of the meaning of love-transformed-justice, or of which individual rights men have they should exercise or not exercise in the order of charity. Not only would justice falter but charity, also, without the challenge to covenant which shows in every

human countenance. Even an act of charity in illum-
inating the meaning of justice and refashioning it more
nearly to the desire at the heart of covenant, and in
determining the exercise or non-exercise of the rights
that men have, needs to have beheld the human countenance of this other man; and thus, also in the order
of charity, natural justice is requisite.

This same thing has to be said in favor of the so-
called "kneel-ins." Besides this there is, in fact, not
much else to be said in their behalf. Of course, on
other grounds the "kneel-ins" as the self-elected creation of community can be defended as well as, or
better than, the self-elected denials of community by
segregation in the church of Jesus Christ, since the in-
troduction of new symbolic or real pressures into the
church no more confuses the kingdoms and instrumen-
talities of this world with the kingdom of God than do
already established and permanently visible, if more
subtle, forms of pressure. But people go to church to
plead only the sacrifice of Christ and His mercy. They
do not go to plead that they are white or black, just or
unjust, sufferers or not from any particular wrong. Nor
do they go to plead the community they have established across racial lines. They go together or separately
to plead only the sacrifice and mercy of Christ, and to
count only on the community that He, the Lord of
Covenant, may create among men. But this means
they go *with,* if only with, the human countenance
lifted up toward God and facing their life with man,
for which and in which they have been called out of
nothing. They cannot go without the inalienable
community not made by human hands, which God

ordained in them as his human creatures, by creating them men who bear in their indestructible humanity (which no man made) the marks of the fact that they were destined for fellow humanity. Pleading only communion with Jesus Christ, they must acknowledge that to all eternity they cannot be men without this fellow man here and now, since Christ is God's resolve from all eternity never to be Lord and God or Man without him.

———

Afterword

The Christian man lives by the grace of God in the order of charity *(agape)*. He lives also by the power and governance of this same God in the order of justice, of natural or human rights, in institutions and under law. These are not totally different orders, nor does charity simply grace the sphere over which justice presides. Rather do charity and justice interpenetrate in various ways.

On the one hand, the order of charity reaches down into the order of justice. It requires the Christian never to do less than what is just, and—as if that were needed—this fixes a gulf between charity and a sentimental love that assumes responsibility to and for only a part of a man (his soul's salvation, perhaps, or for friendship and help to him in the private realm only) and not to and for his whole concrete being, to and for his lifetime in the web of social existence. In this way love affirms his rights. At the same time, it confirms for him rights that may be placed in considerable doubt if his being and his good are sought to be defined only in terms of natural justice as this has to be understood in his special social context or in legal tradition at any moment. Charity is not concerned only with the achievement of minimum rights, at present envisioned—however distant even this goal may be—but with elevating the meaning of justice for every man in every way that it is possible for this to be done, together and in general (as by definition justice must be done in institutions and by law). The order of charity thus interpenetrates the order of justice—affirming and confirming justice and fundamental rights as first and also required of a Christian by the saving love of Christ by whom we and all men have been first loved, and then elevating, transforming, definitely shaping, and fashioning what justice may mean, if possible, more in the direction of the requirements of charity. This entire movement of charity into justice may be termed "faith effective through in-principled love."

On the other hand, the order of justice reaches up to the order of charity, submitting to its final review every judgment and proposed action based only on what "nature itself teaches" or what society and its present laws require. For this reason, e.g., "the law of the land," much less local ordinances not yet tested higher in the courts, can never be allowed to become an absolute criterion. In yet another and perhaps a reverse way, where we suppose that something has been correctly known and said about the rights of man as such, this cannot be for the Christian a final settlement of every issue that may arise for him. The fact that he has a given right does not mean that he can always demand to exercise this right. In addition to trying to determine what justice requires, even the requirement of a love-transformed justice, he may and can and should also ask again what love requires. While most often love will be served best by a fuller exercise of human rights, even as the claim of a Christian for himself, it may be that on occasion renunciation of the claim to exercise the right that he has will be the responsibility of a Christian in the order of charity, not only as an act of a rare and spectacular heroism or the crowning virtue of martyrdom but in the everyday affairs of ordinary men. This may be termed; justice, law, claims, power, rights, virtue, or principles relativized before the Lordship of Christ and bowing down before his Name above every name.

Seeing the mutual interpenetration of the orders of charity and of justice, the Christian searches for the reason for this, and he has not far to seek. He understands the whole range of human life, with or without distinctions, in terms of the ordinance, governance, and direction of the one God known in Jesus Christ. This means there can be for us no final separation between justice and mercy, between what love and nature teach, between nature and grace, between creation and covenant, between God's will hiddenly revealed in His ordinances and God's will revealedly hidden in the Gospel. These alike come to one end; and in each place man is gifted with one purpose: that he should live in indefeasible covenant with God and with man.

A chief problem, however, remains for Christian ethical analysis. This is the question how, in moral decision and action, the Christian's response to God the Creator, his response to God the Ruler and Preserver of this fallen world, and his response to God the Redeemer stand in indivisible relation to each other; and where the stress falls in cases of concrete

decision. The themes employed in undertaking rightly to understand Christian action in race relations are
able to be lifted up to view in an explicit formulation
of Christian social ethics in general, which should then
prove itself in application to other issues as well. This
task cannot be undertaken here. Nevertheless a position can be indicated, which is precisely the theological ethical analysis employed in the foregoing analysis
of the ethical issues involved in the sit-ins and in
other actions to be taken in race relations.

Nature and Christ, creation and covenant, justice
and love—these sources of the Christian's knowledge
of the good and of the content of his moral responsi-
bilities cannot be identified in any way nor separated
from each other. Nor are they to be connected in only
unimportant, incidental, and external fashion. There
is perpetual dialogue between creation and covenant
in the midst of which men stand, and between nature
and Christ as sources for the assessment and illumination of every act of life. Yet it is not enough simply to
say that the relationship is an internal or a dialectical
one. Moreover, the relation is not symmetrical. It rather runs from the anticipations in nature to actualization in Christlike love, and from this with transforming power back to the order of nature. Within the relationship of "Christ transforming natural justice," the
justice we know is still not the same thing as love—
just as nature is not grace or grace nature, and creation is not covenant nor covenant the same as creation,
and anthropology is not Christology nor Christology
anthropolgy. I know no better way to summarize the
inner, asymmetrical connection between natural jus-

tice and love than the formulation used at the beginning of this volume: creation and natural justice
are the external possibility and precondition or basis
for covenant, while in covenant is disclosed the inner-
most meaning and God's proper purposeful direction
of creation. To this our analysis of the created destination of property right, and questions of law and order
and of the use of coercion, has constantly returned.
This is simply to say that in Christ all things cohere
—and among these things (which are yet not the same
as Christ, in whom they are grounded), our human
nature as fellow humanity and all the justice there is
among men.

———